GW00579096

Theme Hotels

Imprint

The Deutsche Bibliothek is registering
this publication in the Deutsche
Nationalbibliographie; detailed biblio-
graphical information can be found on
the internet at http://dnb.ddb.de

ISBN 978-3-938780-24-4

© 2007 by Verlagshaus Braun
www.verlagshaus-braun.de

1st edition 2007

Selection of projects: Per von Groote
Editorial staff: Franziska Nauck,
                      Corinna Schroeder,
                      Stephan Goetz
Final editing: Anna Hinc
Translation: allround Fremd-
                      sprachen GmbH
                      Cord von der Lühe
Graphic design: Michaela Prinz
Reproduction: LVD Gesellschaft
                      für Datenverarbei-
                      tung mbH, Berlin

Per von Groote

Theme Hotels

BRAUN

Contents

Theme Hotels

2 Imprint

4 Contents

6 Foreword

historical ties

10 Mövenpick Hotel Berlin, near Potsdamer Platz | Berlin

16 Hotel Schloss Neuhardenberg | Neuhardenberg

22 Hotel Elephant | Weimar

28 Kloster Hornbach | Hornbach

34 Dorint Sofitel Bayerpost | Munich

40 Widder Hotel | Zurich

mountain pastime

48 Inter Continental Resort Berchtesgaden | Berchtesgaden

54 Hotel Madlein | Ischgl

60 Park Hotel Waldhaus | Flims

66 Romantic-Hotel Chesa Grischuna | Klosters

72 Riders Palace | Laax

78 Hotel Misani | St. Moritz

84 Hotel Castell | Zuoz

designed spaces

92 Arte Luise Kunsthotel | Berlin

98 Pflaums Posthotel | Pegnitz

104 Aenea Designhotel | Wörthersee

110 Augarten Hotel | Graz

116 Style Hotel Vienna | Vienna

122 Der Teufelhof | Basel

128 The Hotel | Lucerne

luxury residences

136 The Regent | Berlin

142 The Westin Bellevue | Dresden

148 Hotel Imperial | Vienna

154 Hotel Eden Roc | Ascona

160 Mandarin Oriental Hotel du Rhône | Geneva

166 Victoria-Jungfrau Grand Hotel & Spa | Interlaken

172 Lausanne Palace & Spa | Lausanne

178 Hôtel des Trois Couronnes | Vevey

wellness islands

186 Yachthafenresidenz Hohe Düne | *Rostock-Warnemünde*

192 Zur Bleiche Resort & Spa | *Burg im Spreewald*

198 Hotel Landhaus Wachtelhof | *Rotenburg*

204 Rogner Bad Blumau Hotel & Spa | *Bad Blumau*

210 Schwarzer Adler | *Kitzbühel*

216 La Réserve Hotel & Spa | *Geneva*

222 Lenkerhof Alpine Resort | *Lenk im Simmental*

228 Therme Vals | *Vals*

urban hideouts

236 Atlantic Hotel Galopprennbahn | *Bremen*

242 Inn Side Premium Hotel | *Bremen*

248 Bristol Hotel | *Frankfurt*

254 Radisson SAS Hotel | *Frankfurt*

260 The Westin Leipzig | *Leipzig*

266 Arabella Sheraton Bogenhausen | *Munich*

272 Hotel Restaurant Ritzi | *Munich*

278 Hotel Drei Raben | *Nuremberg*

284 Zauberlehrling | *Stuttgart*

countryside hotels

292 Hotel Elisabeth von Eicken | *Ahrenshoop*

298 Dorint Sofitel Söl'ring Hof | *Sylt*

304 Landhaus Stricker | *Sylt*

310 Hanner Restaurant Hotel Meetingpoint | *Mayerling*

316 Hotel Seerose Elements | *Meisterschwanden*

322 Hotel Palafitte | *Neuchâtel*

328 Architects Portraits (selection)

333 Hotel Index

334 Picture Credits / Further Participants

All people are equal when they are away from home. This idea may seem a little too

Foreword

Theme Hotels

moralistic, yet it is no less true for that.

Every person is a foreigner when removed from his or her "habitual" environment. In our modern times this has long since ceased to be the exception that proves the rule: on the contrary, it is expected that people will journey, will visit foreign lands. The travelling salesman – the historical figure of the useful outsider – lives on in the form of the modern employee who takes on all the tasks and jobs that require from him an absence of personal ties. It may be one's fate to be foreign, yet foreignness also represents potential, a resource and not least adventure, since it can never become part of what is habitual, part of the local habitat. The guest who stays will soon cease to be an outsider. Whether this is desirable or not is a completely separate issue – especially in the eyes of those extending the hospitality.

The Western world has witnessed the evolution of a hotel trade that is a far cry from the traditional guest-house culture of yesteryear. This new hotel industry has come to lay increasing value on anticipating the wishes of its foreign guests.

This came about in a variety of ways. The first luxury

All people are equal when they are away from home.

hotels, popular amongst the rich and powerful people of the day, appeared from the end of the 18th century onwards in urban centers of culture and spa towns on the threshold of their respective heydays. To a select few they offered untold splendour and a unique degree of luxury. They were meeting place, holiday resort and refuge under one roof – unmatched in their standards of charm and service yet also very much a replication of everything that well-to-do guests, for reasons of practicality, could not take with them on holiday. These guests were to be allowed to feel at home in the strange environment. This qualitative distinction, enhanced by the historic quality of the various establishments, remains an important factor in the high profile enjoyed by these luxury hotels.

What mass tourism has meant for large travel organisations so the globalisation of the world economy has meant for a hotel sector specialising in a business clientele. Slogans with a strange air of cynicism about them were devised: the commercial nomad returned to the steppe and went energetically about his business and all the foreign hostelry had to do was provide a bed and some washing facilities.

With the collapse of social barriers and increased access not only to prosperity but also to riches, and with the advent of the kind of retreats associated with this more affluent group, increasing numbers of foreign travellers came to expect more than simply spartan accommodation, however functional it might also be. The designing of hotels – itself influenced to a large extent by foreigners – came to focus more on the guests' own lifestyle, with the result that the good taste associated with the establishments was soon having an impact across the sector and becoming crucial to the hotel industry as something that could be discussed and debated.

Our perception of our own lifestyle altered as spending on consumer goods expanded in the fifties and sixties.

The broadening of our style horizons was reflected in magazines whose sole function was to give concrete expression to our newly awoken needs. We have internalised the individual and psychological elements of our living environment and acknowledge it also as a symbol of social status. At first it was physiological elements such as comfort and the functionality of objects that dictated the things money was spent on, but in the eighties and nineties ecological and health concerns took over as the main factors in the decision-making process. Now, when we travel, we pack our new taste sensibilities along with the rest of our baggage, setting out from home with or without a fixed idea of what we hope to encounter in terms of accommodation. Our choice of hostelry, however, – our temporary home from home – is seldom left to chance.

In their design and architecture hotels differ widely in their attempts to stand out that extra bit and thus attract the foreign visitor. Prediction of living patterns and preferences begins with the architects and investors and local authorities as they attempt to anticipate how foreign guests live and would like to live and should live in order that they feel encouraged to return to the same hotel in the future. The resulting visions demand sensitivity and courage from the architects and designers. The sheer variety of hotel designs, concepts and themes reflects the hotel's position at the hub of many activities: a hotel is gastronomy, wellness, event management and a congress center in one, yet each area can have its own specific aura. At the same time the setting, the location, and opposition of city and countryside, of seascapes and views over snowy rooftops, of history and the present day, of opulent luxury and modern design, of wellness and business activities all are distinctions in themselves and bring their separate qualities to the overall experience. The question facing the hotelier is not whether he can combine all these themes equally in one package but rather what tones he will seek to set, how he would like to convey them and which spatial design concept he should use in achieving his vision. Astonishing in all this is how each hotel manages, in it's unique way, to make us forget our foreignness. And this is all it can do; we will always be outsiders because we will always be passing through.

A hotel can achieve this by blotting out our awareness of our outsider status and by creating an environment that is alien in another direction. For some guests the rooms and locations may be absurd, for others they may be extraordinary. One thing they are, however, is mind-expanding works of architecture and art that indulge outsiders in the full extent of their otherness, since they cannot be conspicuous – or be the subject of generali-

sations – when viewed against a background of scenes and scenery that lie outside their "habitual" spectrum. In the protective individuality of the hotel the outsider guest can by turns relax and be inspired.

A hotel's individual character assists him in this. It is not simply that the design and architecture of the hotel can suggest a parallel world to the guest; the unique character of the hotel itself, too, is instrumental in dissolving borders. It represents temporal and spatial distance from day-to-day life, the deliberate suspension of mundane imperatives. In the enclave that is the hotel industry service and hospitality adapt themselves to the needs of the guests. For their part the guests choose their accommodation on the basis of these needs, accommodation that demonstrates its distinctive character either by focussing on themes or by benefiting from the impressions gained by third parties – in the absence of which the distinctions still, naturally, remain intact.

What is extraordinary, indeed paradoxical about the situation in which hotel guests find themselves is precisely the fact that their very outsider status has a liberating effect on them. All guests are equally foreign and thus able to savour the different qualities of a host location which is extending to them equal measures of hospitality and an undifferentiated lack of prejudice.

Per von Groote

historical

ties

Hotel Berlin,
Hornbach
el Weiserpost

oss
denberg
ant Weimar
otel Zurich

Architecture and Design:
Architektur & Designbüro Pia M. Schmid, Zurich | IDA 14, Karsten Schmidt-Hoensdorf, Zurich
Builder-owner:
GBI Berlin, www.gbi-berlin.de

above:
Reception
below:
Conference foyer in basement with water lenses as lights

Berlin

The building was erected in two phases in 1913 and 1930 by the Siemens company and

Mövenpick Hotel Berlin,
near Potsdamer Platz

is located across from the Anhalter Bahnhof rail station. An innovative colour and interiors scheme was executed in 2004 to form a new complex that integrates the historically-listed Siemenshöfe courtyards to create a new Mövenpick hotel. The four courtyards are interconnected via a bridge platform and define a unique spatial heart for the complex. Two of the courtyards enclose peaceful oasis-like spaces for the conference area. The second courtyard was fore-seen as a piazza with restaurant spaces and Mediterranean atmosphere. This space is characterised by a glass roof that can be opened and the kitchen space which is open to views from the restaurant seating area. Generously dimensioned door portals lead into the high, lofty rooms. The glass block walls of the bathrooms and the industrial facade plates used in the entrance area reinterpret the industrial character of the original building. Olivewood furniture, full colours, and flowing textiles create a striking contrast to the industrial elements. In the Siemenssaal meeting hall both worlds are brought together to create an atmosphere that enlivens the unique historic spaces with new uses.

11

above:
Siemenshall
mid:
Yard of silence

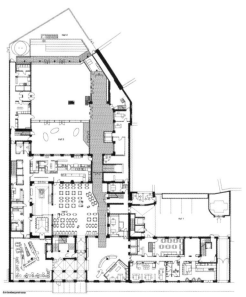
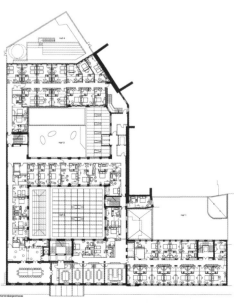

below left:
Ground floor
below right:
Ground plan of 1st floor with
historic Siemenshall

above:
Anhalter Bar with high
voltage isolators
below:
Restaurant "yard 2" with
glass roof

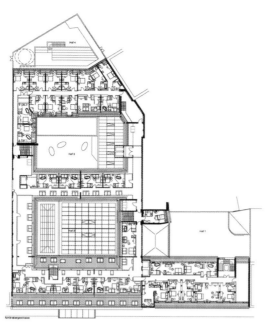

left and right:
Guest room
above right:
Ground plan 5th floor

Architecture:
Lindner Architects,
Düsseldorf
(formerly Lindner-
Roettig-Klasing)
planning and
construction
management,
space extension
Outdoor Facilities:
Gräfin Adelheid von
Schönborn, Munich

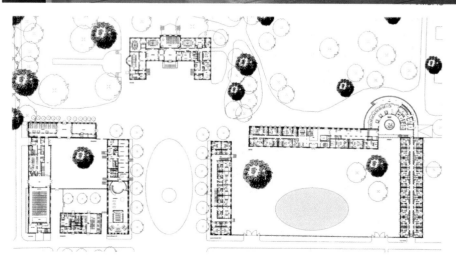

above:
View into the castle
below:
Plan of castle grounds
right:
Breakfast terrace
with view of park

16

Neuhardenberg

Hotel Schloss Neuhardenberg

The three-winged Baroque complex of an earlier era underwent major modifications following its

gifting to the Prussian Chancellor, Karl August Prince Hardenberg. No less an architect than Karl Friedrich Schinkel presided over the extension work, which involved construction of the two-storey classical palace. The outlying buildings, destroyed in a fire, were rebuilt by Schinkel to his own designs. The 1820s saw the laying down of the Baroque parklands in accordance with plans drawn up by Peter Joseph Lenné. It was only thanks to careful preservation and modernisation of the closed complex that present-day owners were able to turn the premises to their current use. Following comprehensive planning, a five-year period of restoration and drastic modifications to the original structure and grounds the site was taken over in Spring 2002 by the Schloss Neuhardenberg Foundation, which operates it as a hotel and a center for arts and culture, sciences and ethics of economy. Guests have at their disposal 50 rooms and two Mansion Suites, all of which emanate a restrained elegance and provide an oasis of peace and restfulness. Classical cuisine, with the accent on Mediterranean dishes, only goes to confirm the Hotel as an establishment of the finest quality.

left:
Castle and park
above:
Library
mid:
Garden room

below:
Hassberg room

above:
Reception
below:
Restaurant "Lenné"

above:
Castle
mid:
Castle by night

below:
Park

Architecture (historical): Hermann Giesler
Architecture (new): Frischgesell + Partners
Interior Design: Bost Berlin Interior Design Architecture, Tassilo Bost

above:
Exterior view
below:
Reception

Weimar
Hotel Elephant

Goethe, Schiller and Hebbel are just three of the celebrities who have stayed at the

Elephant in the course of the Hotel's 300-year-old presence on the historic market square of Weimar. Thomas Mann considered it "an honour and a pleasure" to be the first to sign the guest book when the establishment reopened in 1955. The owners returned the compliment by naming after him a suite that boasts wenge and teak furniture, oak parquet floors and matching sandy-hued materials and fabrics. The suite's baths are of Saalburg and Botticino marble decorated with etched glass illustrations. The other suites also bear the names of famous people: as recently as November 2004 the 3rd-floor Lilli Palmer Suite was inaugurated in honour of the actress Lilli Palmer, star of the 1975 film "Lotte in Weimar". Each suite is associated with its own references to the person whose name it bears: a library of Thomas Mann books, for instance, can be found directly across from its namesake suite. In the spacious lobby Art Deco elements are reflected in the marble floor and gleaming, black surfaces. The Marlene Bar is pure Art Deco, with green glass and black wood and wenge surfaces predominating.

above:
Lobby
mid:
Bar "Marlene"

below:
Lobby

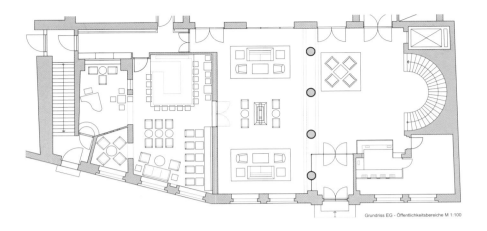

Grundriss EG - Öffentlichkeitsbereiche M 1:100

above:
Ground plan of ground floor
public area
below:
Restaurant "Anna Amalia"

above:
Dining / sleeping area of
Thomas Mann suite
below:
Ground plan of
1st floor / suites

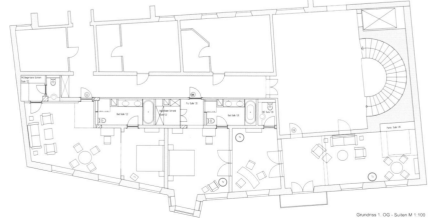

Grundriss 1. OG - Suiten M 1:100

26

above:
Living area of
Thomas Mann suite

below:
Suite bathroom

Architecture:
Meckler + Partners
Interior Design:
Flum Design

above:
Cloisters
below:
Foyer
right:
Fragments of the
eastern cloisters

28

Hornbach

The same location chosen by the Benedictine monk Pirminius as the site for a monastery

Kloster Hornbach

is now host to the Kloster Hornbach Hotel, nestling on its plateau in the countryside. The privileges enjoyed by the monastery, lying as it did close to the French border, allowed it to prosper at first, but the centuries took their toll. Wars, plague and religious conflicts ushered in a period of decline and the monastery fell into ruin. Not until excavations had been carried out could the old complex be transformed into the unique hotel we see today, a rebirth also made possible by the architects' and owners' sensitive treatment of the historic structure during restoration work. The Gothic building has traditional materials contrasting daringly, if decently, with glass and steel. The spare, Shaker style subtly highlights the particularities of the structure without sacrificing modern comforts and state-of-the-art technology. From the Monastery's ancient herb garden, inviting visitors to tarry and unwind, to the light, French cuisine of the Hotel's own restaurant: this is a setting that is guaranteed to relax and inspire its guests.

above:
Remise and beer garden
mid:
Event room "Wedding"
above right:
Vaults of restaurant

below:
Philosopher's room
below right:
Ground plan of monastery
tavern, entrance and chapel

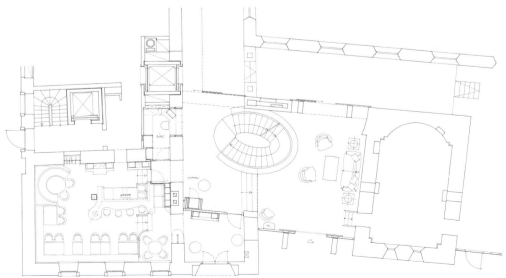

above:
Resting room "BathPleasure"
mid:
Relaxing pool "BathPleasure"
above right:
Ethno-style room

below left:
Wedding suite "ForEver"
and mediterranean room
below right:
Shakerroom and
ground plan shakerroom

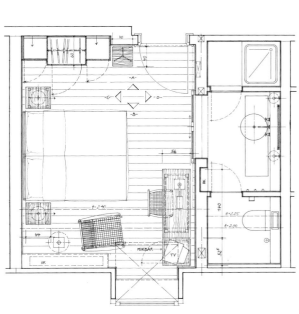

Architecture:
Architecture Practice
Prof. Fred Angerer
and Gerald Hadler,
Munich
Interior Design:
Klein / Haller,
Mönchengladbach

above:
Eastern side
below:
Facade detail
right:
Ground plans ground floor,
1st floor and longitudinal section

Munich
Dorint Sofitel Bayerpost

The former royal Bavarian main post office in Munich built from 1896–1900 stood empty and

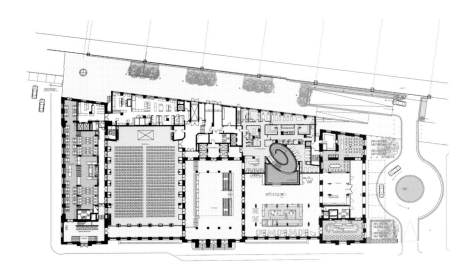

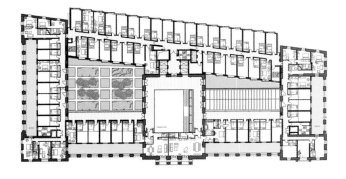

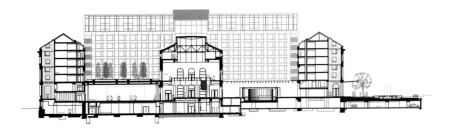

unused for several years. Post-war alterations hid the characteristic steel structural elements from view and reduced the height of the original spaces. The marginal, subordinate north wing of the building was replaced by a new building. The original interior spatial composition was re-constructed with regard to historic preservationist concerns. This was achieved by inserting a new interior facade that is recessed behind the historic facade. The existing natural stone facades in Italian High Renaissance style were refurbished and the historic hull encloses a modern core. The in-between spaces create a clear break within which the linear, glossy, and clear interior architecture exists. Natural materials were implemented: shell limestone, leather, Indian slate, bronze mosaics, and Rosso-Levanto marble create an exciting sequence of light and dark zones. The captivating spatial sequence which leads guests from the bright entrance to the theatrically staged reception area via the 18 meter high light sculpture beneath the glass roof forms the central element of the interior design concept.

left:
Library
above:
Lobby with light sculpture
mid:
Wellness area

below:
Public restroom

above:
Presidential suite
mid:
Bed detail
right:
Restaurant Suzie W

below:
Bathroom

Architecture:
Tilla Theus and
Partners,
Tilla Theus
Implementation:
Karl Steiner AG

above:
Courtyard as resting area
below:
Main entrance
right:
Reception of restaurant

40

Zurich
Widder Hotel

The Widder Hotel in Zurich's Old Town is spread over eight restored private townhouses

that have been linked into a single ensemble while retaining their own distinct characters within and without. The aim here was to identify features worth preserving and integrate them into the whole. Six core structures dating back to the Middle Ages were restored in their entirety. Among the features discovered in the excavation process were parts of a Roman road, the remains of a settlement from the 12th century BC and an ancient fire site. Issues of conservation coupled with the existing building materials, forms and structures presented architects with a challenge and a welter of design possibilities. Despite this they have succeeded in producing a homogenous entity by exploiting similarities in the buildings' materials and lines and their unobtrusive, natural shades. The vibrancy of the interior spaces comes from the contrasts and dialogue between old and new. One example here is the juxtaposition of stone wall with incorporated metal structure, as in the case of the seven-storey staircase in the rear of the building at No. 3, Rennweg. Each of the 42 rooms and seven suites has its own layout and design, its own colours and its own unique furnishings and fittings.

41

left:
Fireplace
above:
Library of spirits, widder jazz
bar and round foyer

below:
Light yard as junction

above:
Hotel room 209
mid:
Layout plan – the eight
houses of the medieval center

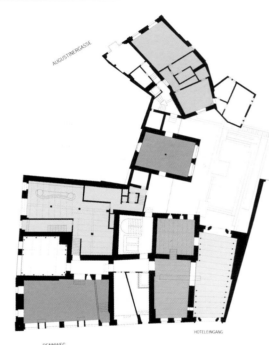

below:
Hotel room furnished with
modern classics
right:
Old panelling with historic
fitted wardrobe

mountain

pastime

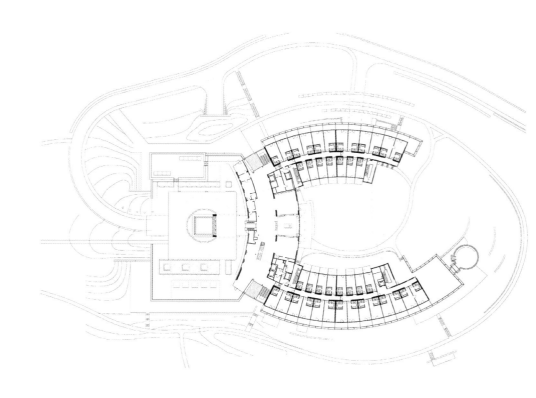

Architecture:
Kochta Architects,
Herbert Kochta
Interior Design:
Mahmoudieh Design,
Berlin |
Sporer Plus,
Stuttgart
**Revision and
Current Design:**
DBLB Architects,
Munich,
Dr. André Behncke

above:
Exterior view
below:
Ground floor with driveaway,
terrace floor with junior suites
and cross section
right:
View of the terrace,
Kehlstein in backround

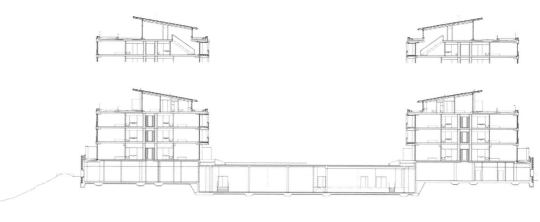

Berchtesgaden InterContinental Resort

The Berchtesgaden resort is embedded in the natural mountainside setting and commands

impressive views out over pristine Alpine landscapes. The building organisation takes the unique site into account: the three-storied room wings huddle into the hillside topography, and the plinth level, clad in natural stone, merges with the mountain. Green roofs allow the buildings to naturally merge with the Alpine surroundings. Room-high glazing in the rooms and suites creates an open atmosphere. The foyer hall on the northern edge of the complex interconnects the room wings to create an open courtyard to the south. The ground floor contains social functions such as the reception area, bar, lounge by the fireplace, and library. The interior architecture utilises high-quality materials to create clearly modern aesthetics. The exterior natural stone wall extends into the lobby, parquet flooring made of smoked oak was used in the rooms, and the Verde Dolomit stone used in the bathrooms contrasts with the dark wooden sheathing of the bathtubs. Open fireplaces in the rooms make them warm and inviting.

above:
Lobby
below:
Library

50

above:
Anteroom of Le Ciel
and winery
below:
3'60° restaurant & grill
with view of show kitchen

above left:
Living room of
presidential suite
mid:
Bathroom of
presidential suite
above right:
Standard deluxe room

below left:
The Mountain Spa
below right:
Outdoor swimming pool

Architecture:
Mescherowsky
Architects
(extension wellness
area and suites)
Interior Design:
Sabine Mescherowsky

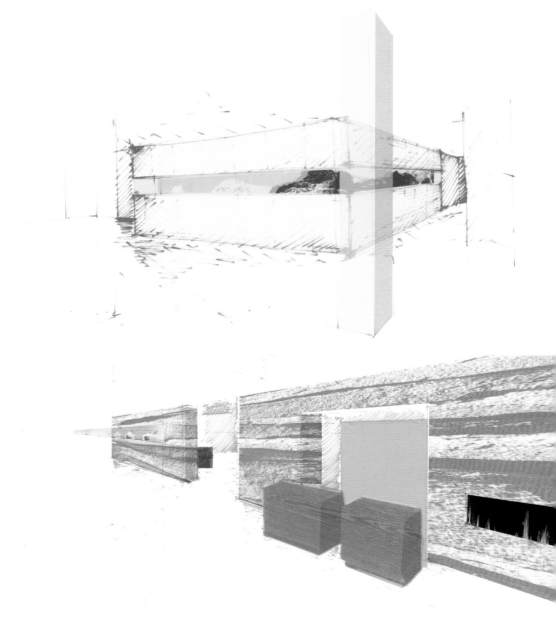

above:
Extension
wellness area / suites
below:
Sketches of alps panorama
and natural stone wall
right:
Lobby

Jschgl
Hotel Madlein

The Madlein Hotel has opted for a simple, purist design that keeps faith with the character of the region: loden and calf coat have both been employed in a number of instances and a log fireplace crackles in the lobby. The Alpine panorama using LED light needs no elaboration. Quiet alcoves in the lobby contrast with the public areas, as do the materials with the colour schemes – walls consisting of large, beige limestone plates are in stark opposition to the deep-pile mocha brown carpet. The lighting arrangement reflects the time of day either indirectly or as a mock-celestial representation. As a forum for encounters and rendezvous the bar is very much the focal point of the Hotel: the reception desk, the restaurant, the wellness area, the club in the basement and the staircase down from the rooms all lead to it. The bar's oval counter, built of bog oak and lit from below, stands diagonally to the lie of the room. Bar stools of dark brown leather assert their independence from the body of the counter, with its beige plaster ostrich egg look. The points of light on the bar play on the multicoloured drinks, the faces at the bar appearing suffused in shadow.

left:
Ascent to suites
above:
Alps panorama
mid:
Fireplace with calf coat stools

below:
Idea sketch of lounge / bar

above and mid:
Suite
above right:
Bar

left:
Wellness area
right:
Idea sketch bar

Architecture and Design:
Architektur & Designbüro Pia M. Schmid, Zurich |
Architecture Practice Hans Peter Fontana, Flims
Lighting Plan Wellness Area:
Lichtkompetenz Krewinkel, Jörg Krewinkel

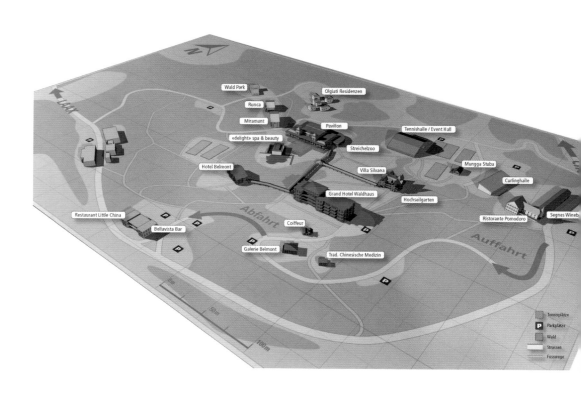

above:
Aerial view
below:
Site map and section
right:
View of the pavilion

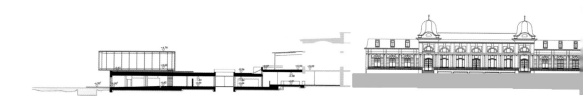

Flims
Park Hotel Waldhaus

The existing hotel complex was completely refurbished. The newly renovated rooms of the

Grand Hotel Waldhaus now stand for noble materials, clear forms, warm earthy colours, and timeless elegance and such create a marked contrast to the former feudal Grand Hotel Style. The refurbishment measures on the Villa Silvana retained its unique Jugendstil charm. The design intention of creating austere, simple details and spaces that are at the same time comfortable and welcoming was consequently realised on all four building levels. The pavilion social hall dating from the turn of the century was restored to its original opulence, including the southern facade with the adjoining spacious promenade and restaurant terrace. The glass cube of the covered pool building reflects the mountain scenery during the daytime and glows like a lantern at night thanks to lighting integrated in the floors. The subterranean wellness facilities seem transparent and, due to the natural stone surfaces utilised here and all through the hotel, naturally embedded in the earth. Adobe walls that naturally regulate the interior climate, colourful rendering of the free-standing sauna cubes, and cherry wood details create well placed accents.

above:
Lit up wellness building
"delight" spa & beauty
mid:
Idyllic swimming pond
above right:
Ground plan ground floor

below left:
Resting room with ambiance
below right (f. l. t. r.):
Sauna and bistro-cafe
"The Lounge"

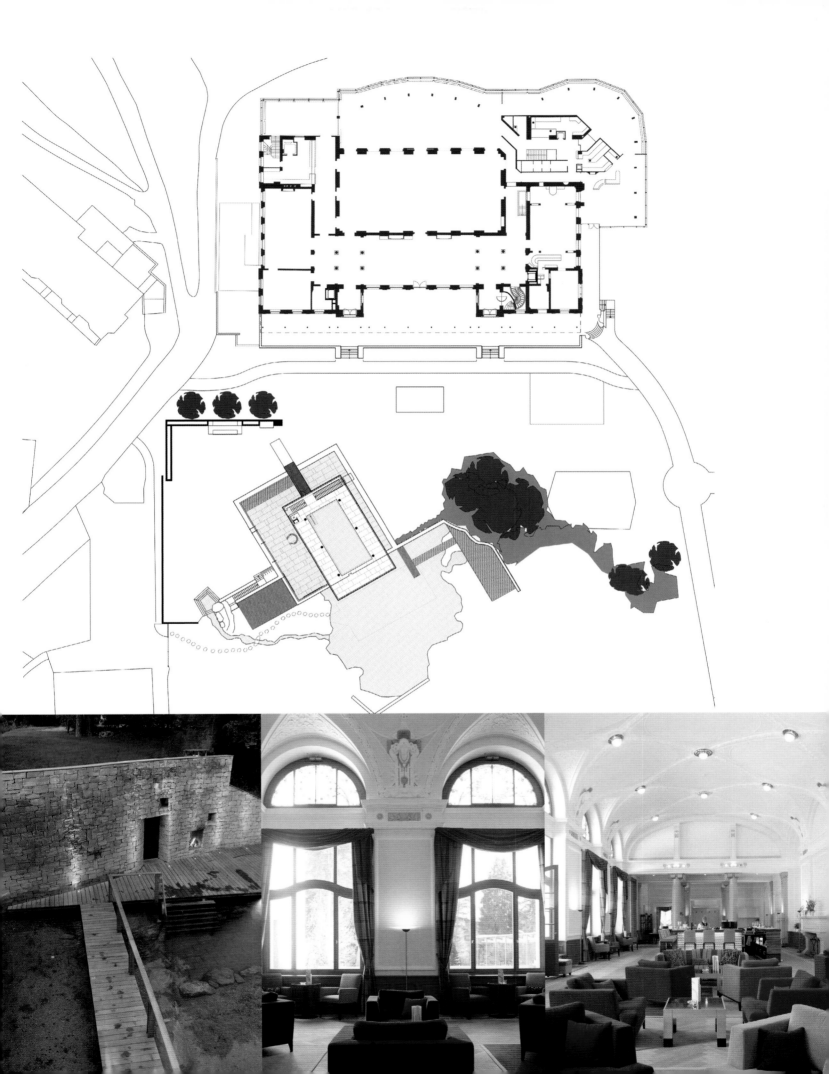

left:
Modern rooms in timeless elegance; clear forms and precious materials

right:
The rooms of the art nou-
veau villa Silvana, renovated
in the style of a summer
residence

Architecture and
Interior Design:
Hermann Schneider

Klosters
Romantic-Hotel Chesa Grischuna

The 1892 "Alpina" guesthouse that once stood on the same site at the heart of one of the most popular Alpine ski resorts was replaced in 1938 by the Chesa Grischuna complex. After razing of the original structure, the architect Hermann Schneider was given complete artistic freedom for the design of the building organisation, interiors, and facades of the hotel and restaurant. The down-to-earth comfortable atmosphere present in all of the spaces is the result of his singular artistic concept. The project was executed in an era in which special was given to traditional regional construction methods, a fact that was evidenced at the concurrent State Exhibition held in Zurich. Solely local workers crafted the wooden elements and metalwork foreseen for the windows and doors. Even the curtains and silverware were designed as integral parts of the overall concept. Noted contemporary artists of the time such as Hans Schoellhorn and Alois Cariget were commissioned to create frescoes, wall paintings, and paintings on wood. Today, ownership in the second generation lovingly preserves a special place that has lured Hollywood celebrities and European high nobility to stay and dine in Klosters.

above left:
The legendary
Chesa-restaurant

above right:
Small patio at the
main entrance

below:
Regulars table

above left, mid and right:
Guest rooms

below left:
Staircase
below right:
Wooden decoration
elements

Architecture:
René Meierhofer,
Laax
**Construction
Management:**
Richard Schneller,
Trin
Housing Technology:
Hans Hermann,
Planning and
Advisory Office, Chur
Lighting Plan:
Zumtobel Staff
Switzerland, Zurich

above:
Exterior view
left:
Detail of facade

Laax
Riders Palace

The architecture of Riders Palace is urban, cube-like, and undecorated. A select palette of materials such as concrete, wood, and large-format glazing are combined to form building masses that also create striking lighting effects. At night, the transparent surfaces of the building hull project interior scenes out from the "containers" to the exterior. The lighting scheme creates a unique ambience both within suites and in the central lobby space that can be seen from all floors and houses a 24-hour bar on the ground floor. Translucent glass surfaces that shimmer in changing colours were used on the bar, for cabinets, or as movable walls in the suite bathrooms. A 1.000 m² large space is located on two subterranean levels. The well-known music club located here has an austere charm and assumes different lighting and acoustical atmospheres with the changing events that take place here. Sustainable technology was implemented in the design of all technical installations. Energy for heating via a heat pump is acquired from a nearby reservoir. As a result of the creative combination of innovative sustainable technologies the complex was awarded the "Minergie" label for buildings that consume less than 45 kilowatts / m² per year.

above left and mid:
View of the bar
above right:
Lobby

below left:
Lobby and bar
below right:
Ground floor plan
and eastern view

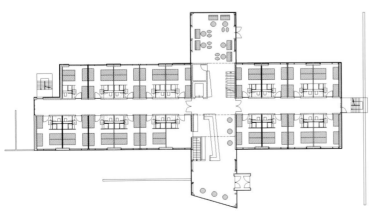

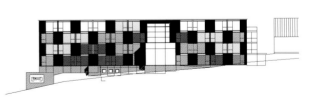

0-05

above and mid:
View into room

below:
Section

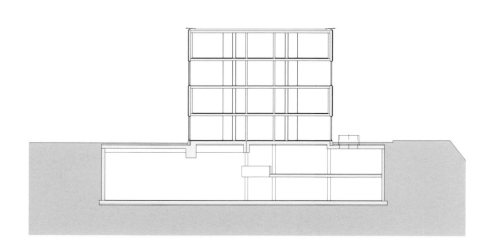

above and mid:
Suite with bathroom

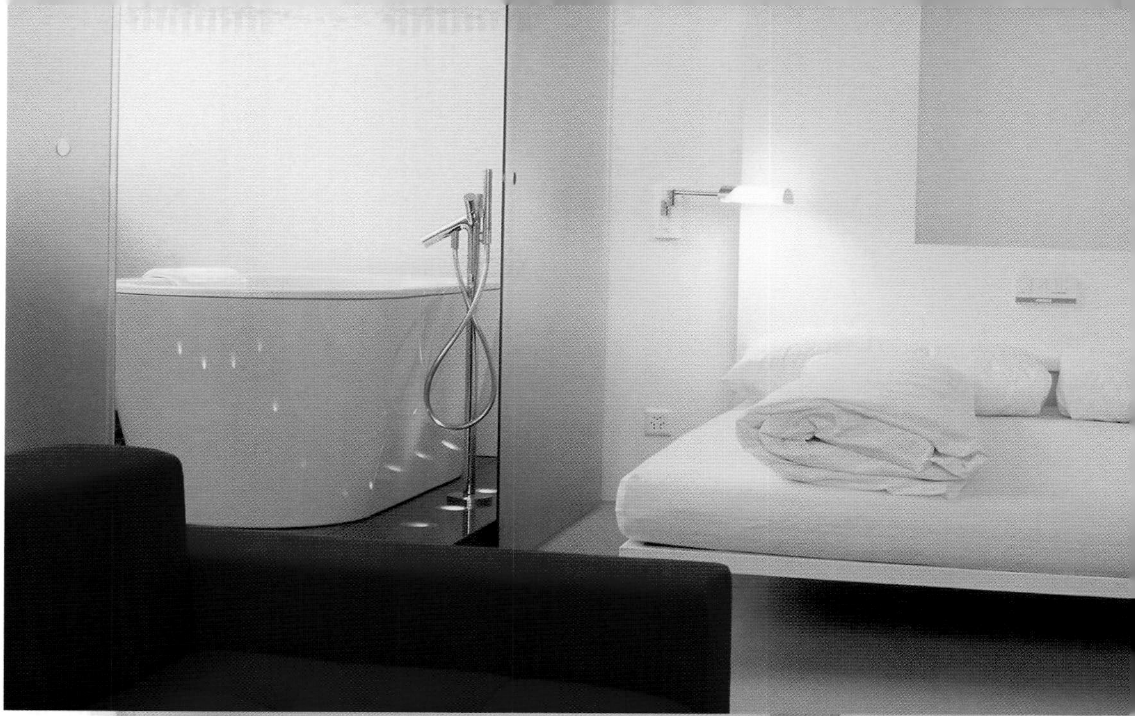

below:
Room

Architecture:
Kurt Lazzarini
**Interior Design
Ground Floor:**
Edoardo Coretti,
Muralto | Zurich

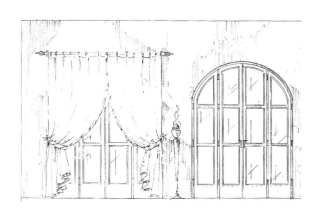

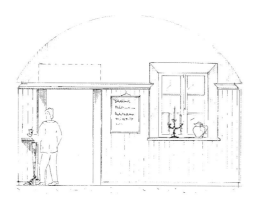

above:
Exterior view
below:
Views of Bodega wine cellar /
tapas bar and restaurant
right:
General equipment, guests may
embellish their rooms

St. Moritz

Hotel Misani

This building reminiscent of Northern Italy, a symmetrically designed, late-Classical cube with structured flat roof, was completely refurbished following a plethora of unco-ordinated operations on the facade and roof. For the over-haul a simple, unadorned interpretation of the original 1878 building was chosen. A heavily pigmented, earthy colour was chosen for the facade to emphasie the open-ness of the design and the Italian influence prevalent at the time. The communal areas of the hotel are a blend of Engadin and Mediterranean influences. The original wood panelled rooms on the ground floor now do service as the Ustaria Misani Restaurant. Behind the doors of the 'Style Rooms', with their evocative names, lie oases of calm dec-orated in warm and refreshing watercolours. The artistically designed rooms all have their own interesting details such as the sword fish sculpture on the wall of the Kava'i Room or the suspended, rear-lit ceiling pictures with their motifs from Siam and Kyoto.

above left:
Bodega Misani with lounge
mid:
Bodega Misani tapas
restaurant
above right:
Bodega Misani tapas bar

below left:
Fireplace
below right:
View of the bar

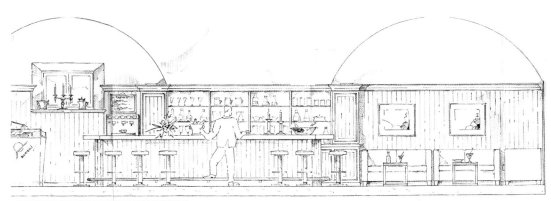

above:
Room Agadir – Marocco
mid:
Room Timbuktu – Mali

below:
Room Medina – Saudi Arabia

above:
Room Chihuauha – Mexico
mid:
Room Havana – Cuba
below:
Room Agrar – India

Architecture and Interior Design:
UN Studio
Ben van Berkel
with Olaf Gipser

above:
Hillside situation
of the buildings
below:
Exterior view of old
and new hotel building

84

Zuoz
Hotel Castell

The old Hotel Castell Zuoz was built in 1913 by Nicolas Harmann as a health spa hotel. Bought by the Swiss art collector Bechtler in the mid 1990s, the hotel has developed gradually into a modern art and wellness hotel. The most comprehensive period of renovation and extension in the building's history has recently come to an end, with a new modern annexe added adjacent to the original building. All 14 of its open-plan apartments face south and enjoy all the benefits of the hotel's site topography and the services offered by the main body of the Hotel. The glass facade provides a spectacular view over the Engadin Valley. In the cellar of the hotel a Hammam was created, its interior reflecting the classicism of the rest of the building. Five illumination cylinders concentrate a limited amount of light on the central atrium. The 60 hotel rooms have been completely redesigned, the discrete impression of spaciousness harmonising with the Hotel's art works. From the new wooden terrace designed by Japanese artist Kawamata guests can admire art objects and installations in the garden.

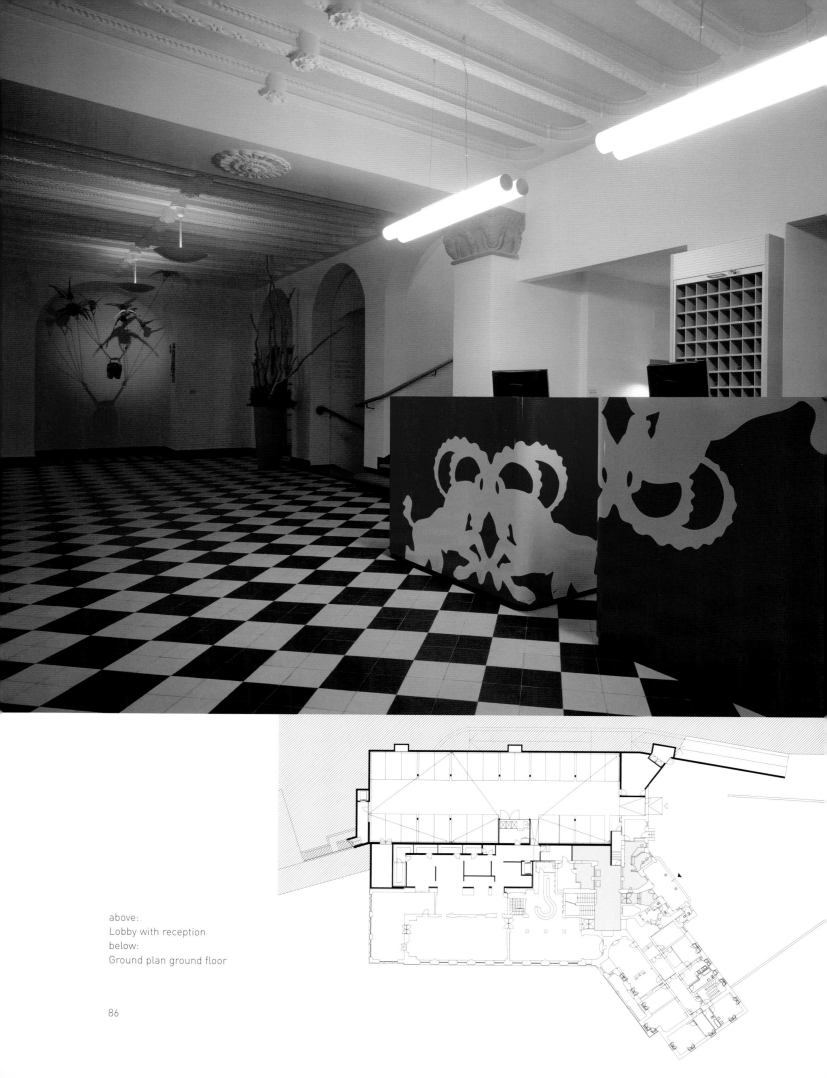

above:
Lobby with reception
below:
Ground plan ground floor

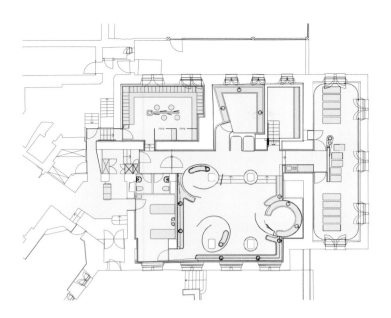

above:
Ground plan hamam
below:
Hamam

above and below:
Alpine purism in the
guest rooms

above left and below:
Pastel colours in the rooms
above right:
Panoramic view
towards the alps

designed

spaces

Architecture:
Rainer Seiferth
**Interior Design
and Art:**
see
www.luise-berlin.com

above:
Exterior of the palais
below:
View from the hotel towards
the government and
parliament buildings

92

Berlin
Arte Luise Kunsthotel

In the fall of 1999, the Arte Luise Kunsthotel (formerly: Künstlerheim Luise) opened

in a historic Neo-classical urban palace dating from 1825. An extension wing was built in 2003 to act as a noise barrier to the adjacent rail lines. The complex has grown from its beginnings as an existentialist living-art-project to a hotel with almost 50 rooms and an art hall within five walking minutes of the Reichstag building. Due to the uniqueness of each room one must stay here more than 50 times in order to experience all of the varied interior worlds. Just as many artists have immortalised themselves in the rooms. Whether in the over-dimensioned oak bed meant to symbolise a happy childhood, or in a collage of airplane parts hug from the ceiling to give one a sense of flying – the guests choice of room plays a major role in creating a memorable stay. The far-eastern, meditative atmosphere of the "Japanese Garden" room allows one to directly experience the pulse of the city: the S-Bahn commuter train runs directly in front of the window, yet remains silent and unheard due to class 6 acoustically insulated windows and air conditioning.

above left:
Room 210 "Heartbeat"
by Kiddy Citny
above right:
Isometry
mid right:
Ground plans

below left:
Room 202 "Samarkand"
by Shukhrat Babajanov
below right (f.l.t.r.):
Hall of art, staircase in the
old building and back
facade of the new building

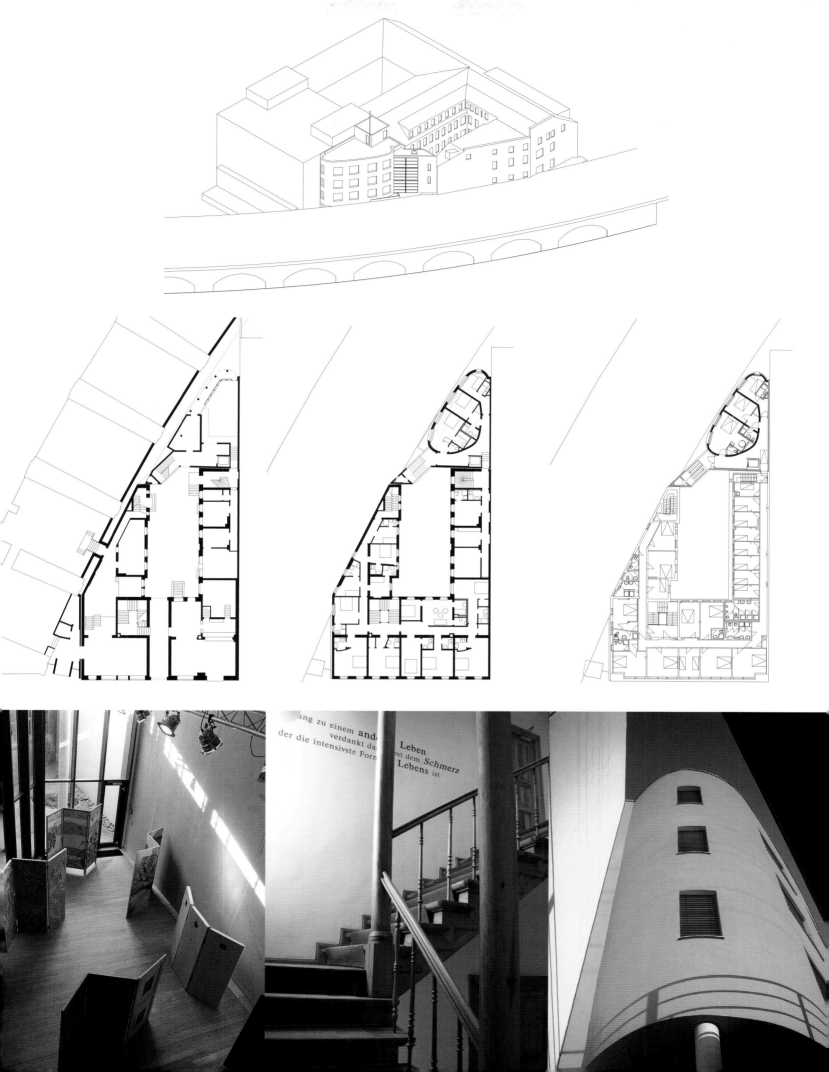

above left:
Room 302 "Panorama 360°"
by Markus Linnenbrink
mid:
Room 208 "Tribute to Edward
Hopper" by Volker März
above right:
Room 102 "Royal Suite"
by the "Bananasprayer"
Thomas Baumgärtel

below left:
Room 300 "The poor poet"
by Andreas Paeslack
below right (f.l.t.r.):
Suite 212 "Innocence"
by Ottmar Hörl,
room 306 "Comic" by KEHL
and room 314 "Under the
red horse" by
Roman Schmelter

Interior Design:
Dirk Obliers |
Andreas Pflaum

below:
Tradition and avantgarde
above and right:
Golf, nature park
Fränkische Schweiz

98

Pegnitz
Pflaums Posthotel

The original structure that housed the name-giving postal station was built in

1707. Thanks to the Pflaums family, currently in the 11th generation, the town Pegnitz has achieved notoriety thanks not only to its Franconian charm. Their hotel has also played a major role in making the place popular with culinary aficionados, politicians, celebrities, and opera fans visiting the nearby Bayreuth opera festival. The interiors are characterised by contrasting spatial scenarios. Blue dominates everything in the "Venus in Blue" suite. Even the floors and ceilings are integrated into the futuristic concept. The austere metal furnishings smoothly merge into the space. The Parsifal suite similarly appeals to the senses. Lighting effects and mirrors create countless sparkling stars, the furniture seems somehow frozen in its multifunctional state and oddly disjointed from its actual use. A more contemplative suite where Napoleon reputedly once stayed was named after the noted guest. The cross-timber wooden framework is exposed here. Red is the dominating colour in the restaurant and the bar where dark the wooden ceiling creates a cosy ambience.

above:
PPP outdoor dining
mid:
Historic postmen's lounge

below:
Restaurant
Pflaumen@Garden
for gourmets and
winelovers

above:
Hall
below:
Traditional and
futuristic interior

above left:
Rosenthal suite "Expo"
mid:
Henry IV suite of gods,
popes, emperors and kings
above right:
Suite Venus in blue

below left:
PPP spa & oasis blue
below right:
Suite Venus in blue

Architecture:
Andreas Krainer
Interior Design:
Sabine
Mescherowsky

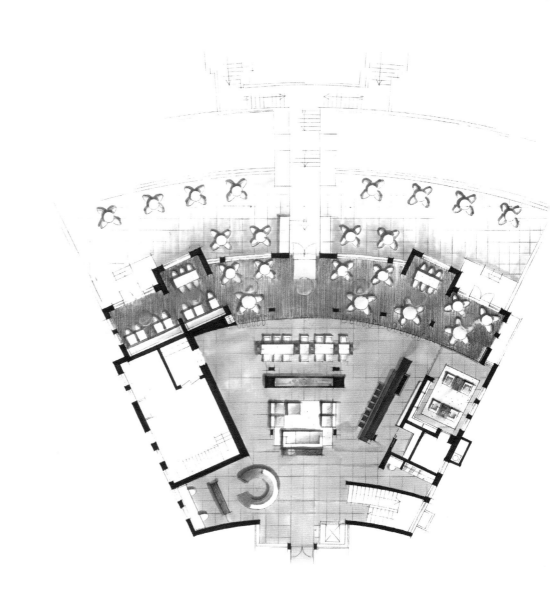

above:
Hotel entrée
below:
Sketch of ground floor
right:
View of entrance / bridge

Wörthersee
Aenea Designhotel

Guests can enjoy the view over the Wörthersee from all parts of the Aenea Design Hotel –

ground floor, suites, wellness area. Around the Kamin Lounge on the ground floor the bar, restaurant and library are arranged as little islands constructed in matching materials and colour scheme. The sweeping greys of the floor, made of stone imported from Pietra Serena, confer a stately ambience on the area, while suffused lighting emanates peacefulness. The restaurant's floor of smoked oak is in striking contrast to the white plaster of the walls. The bar, with its coloured, illuminated glass tower, is a perfect meeting place. Lighting under the counter gives it an appearance of floating. The 6-metre wide open fireplace in the middle of the Kamin Lounge is surrounded by easy chairs. Beige coloured, deep pile carpets in the suites contrast with the severe lines of the furniture. Glass and stone are the main materials to be found in the wellness area, where the lighting scheme bathes individual areas such as the glass swimming pool in their own private ambience.

left:
Restaurant
above:
Library

mid:
Fireplace lounge
below:
Idea sketch bar / fireplace

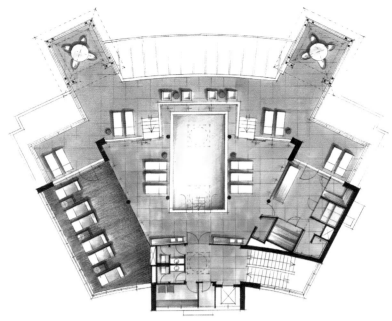

above left:
Ground plan wellness area
mid:
Wellness swimming pool
above right:
Suite

below left:
Wellness swimming pool
below right:
Bathroom suite

Architecture:
Günther Domenig

above:
Roof terrace
below:
Sketch
right:
Lobby

Graz
Augarten Hotel

The Augarten, conceived as an integral, unified designer hotel, lies a few hundred

metres from Graz city center. Against a backdrop of classical residential buildings the architect has created a modern, sober architecture on what is a long, slim plot of land. Facades of glass and the exterior stairs provide a degree of transparency while the façade's slightly tapering surfaces inject a measure of dynamism. The brightness of the staircase core, decked with its pictures by contemporary artists, radiates a lightness in the form of pergolas and light-flooded foyers. The design follows one idea consistently – artistic forms of comfort, comfortable forms of art. There a few details in which one or other of the many artists involved in this hotel project has not had a hand. All areas - from the corridors to the rooftop terrace – double as exhibition spaces. In a hotel that, like its exhibition programme, is in continual evolution, leisure and business travellers alike will all derive their own personal satisfaction from little details of the Hotel and its unique artistic atmosphere.

above:
Outer area and lift
mid:
Staircase

below:
Reception

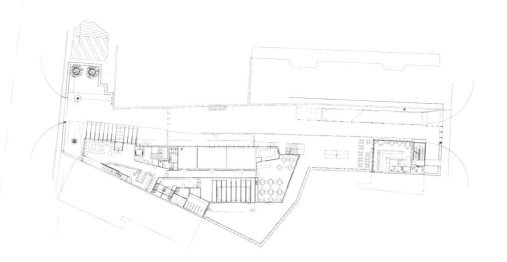

above:
Ground floor plan
below:
Pool

left:
Room 501
above:
Room 410
mid left:
Section

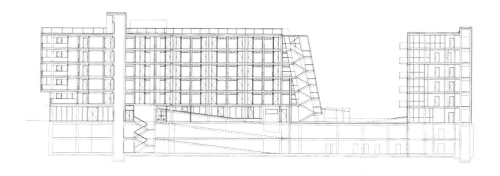

mid right:
Balcony
below:
Room 310

115

Architecture:
Thanner Architects
Interior Design:
MKV Design,
Maria Vafiadis
Project Management:
Andrea
Haselbacher GmbH

above:
Facade
below:
Ground floor plan
right:
Reception

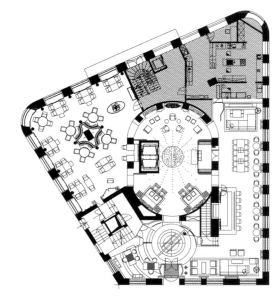

Vienna
Style Hotel Vienna

The Style Hotel, built in the center of Vienna in 2005, is a contemporary interpretation of Vienna's early 1920s Secession Art Nouveau. With the Hotel located at the intersection of four streets it was possible to have all rooms and suites looking outwards. High ceilings and large windows maximise natural light and provide splendid views of the Old Center of Vienna. The Hotel has 600 m² of communal premises arranged around a high atrium. Two lifts links the lobby with the upper floors. A large Art Deco chandelier dominates the center of the foyer. Gold ornaments, glass and subtle lighting feature throughout the hotel. Although the individual rooms vary in size they share certain features – modern, colourful furniture, Italian glass mosaics in the baths and mirrored TV screens. Rounding out the Hotel's perfectly balanced atmosphere are the recurring colours – cream and crimson – and dark wooden, leather and chrome building materials.

left:
Library
above:
Lounge

below:
"Sapori" restaurant

above:
Bathroom
right:
Guest room

below:
Bar H$_2$0

Architecture:
Hans Pösinger, Basel
Artistic Room Design:
Dominique
Thommy-Kneschaurek

below:
Exterior view of culture and
guest house Teufelhof Basel

Basel
Der Teufelhof

Mr and Mrs Thommy-Kneschaurek have channelled their passions for gastronomy,

theatre and art into creating a many-facetted focus of creativity. The accent is firmly on eating and drinking, as evinced by the salon character of the Bel Etage Restaurant, with its fine parquet floor and classical furniture, and the wine bar with adjacent winter garden and sheltered courtyard. The second creative vein is provided by the hotel theatre, with its classical stage and capacity for 100 people in conventional rows of seating salvaged from Zurich's former opera house. Art installations adorn each of the Hotel's nine rooms. Extension work on the Hotel revealed sections of Basel's old city wall dating back to the 11th and 13th centuries; these sections now flank the archaeological cellar and the falstaff wine shop. Every year the rooms of the 'Gallery Hotel' are rehung with works by new artists. The younger part of the building is stocked with furniture by Swiss designer Kurt Thut and the celebrated Italian designers Vico Magistretti and Achille Castiglioni.

above:
Courtyard of wine tavern
mid:
Theatre in Teufelhof with
chairs from Zurich Opera
right:
Detail pointing to wine store
"falstaff"

below:
View of art installation
"library" by Hubertus
Gojowczyk in "Bel Etage"
restaurant

above:
Art room no. 6:
"Thought-labyrinth"
mid:
Art room no. 8:
"Do it yourself-
interpretation of dreams"

below:
Art room no. 7:
"Reflections"

above:
Art room no. 3:
"Dove and Falcon"
mid:
Part of the suite in the
art hotel
below:
Art room no. 4:
"Coming and Going"

Architecture:
Ateliers Jean Nouvel

above:
Lobby
below:
Exterior view by night
right:
Entrance

Lucerne

The Hotel

'The Hotel' is as brash in name as it is unconventional and individualistic in the way it

conveys to its guests the sensations of modern living. Built in 1907, the building has retained its entire, original sandstone façade. Only the high windows afford a glimpse of the interior, which was transformed by star architect Jean Nouvel into a hotel offering 25 splendid rooms and suites spread over seven floors. The lounge design is suggestive of a kind of floating gallery above the restaurant and ground floor. The décor of the rooms and suites appear poly-dimensional owing to their ceiling illustrations, each room's ceiling depicting a scene from a different film. Stark, smooth surfaces dominate the rooms and baths. All vertical faces are of wood, all horizontals are of chrome steel. Every piece of furniture, from the restaurant chairs to the beds, was designed exclusively by Jean Nouvel for the Hotel.

left:
Lounge
above:
Restaurant Bambou,
detail of kitchen

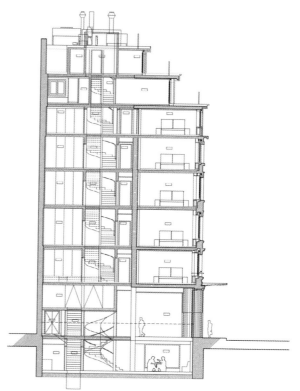

mid:
Section
below:
Ground plan

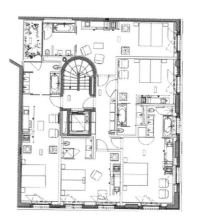

above:
Detail room 5201
below left:
Room 5300
"Al di la delle Antonini"
below right:
Room 5200 "Il casanova"
Federico Fellini
right:
Room 5201 "Matador"
Pedro Almodovar

luxury

residences

Architecture:
Josef Paul Kleihues
Interior Design:
Frank Nicholson

above:
Facade detail
below:
View from
Französische Strasse,
corner Charlottenstrasse

136

Berlin
The Regent

Located in central Berlin just minutes by foot from the Brandenburg Gate, the State Opera, and Unter den Linden boulevard, the light shingle-like Travertine facades of the Regent Berlin rise above the dark green plinth of the ground floor. The hotel is one element of the larger "Hofgarten am Gendarmenmarkt" urban concept developed in 1991 by Josef Paul Kleihues. The seven-storey fronts are characterised by the austere room window openings with French balconies. Two set-back roof levels are enclosed by surrounding balconies. The interior architecture of the 195 luxury rooms, including 39 suites, is timelessly elegant and detailed in the classic design vein. Modern artwork on the walls and valuable antiques complement each other. The Fischers Fritz gourmet restaurant is panelled in wood, decorated with busts, and lit by crystal chandeliers. The restaurant offers fish specialties of the highest culinary quality, served with a view of the historic Gendarmenmarkt square. The elegant interior design was also implemented in the nine variously sized conference spaces.

above:
Entrance Charlottenstrasse
below:
Terrace in courtyard

above left and below:
Salon gontard
above right:
Lobby

above:
Room with a view
mid:
Presidential suite
right:
Linden suite

below:
Bathroom

Architecture:
Johann Georg
Gebhardt
(completed 1727) |
Pfau Architects,
Dresden (building
construction)
Interior Design:
Bost Berlin
Interior Design
Architecture

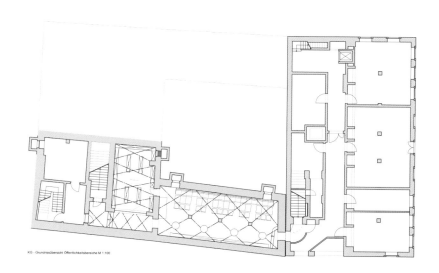

KG - Grundrissübersicht Öffentlichkeitsbereiche M 1:100

above:
Exterior view
below:
Ground plan of basement
and public ground floor
right:
Atrium

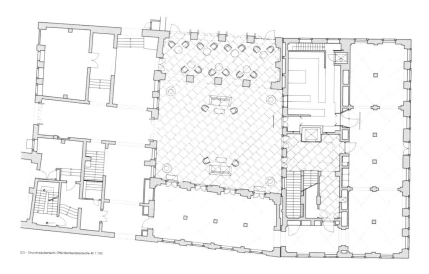

EG - Grundrissübersicht Öffentlichkeitsbereiche M 1:100

142

Dresden
The Westin Bellevue

The redesign of the central, baroque part of the Westin Bellevue involved stripping

three entire floors and creating 14 luxury suites that combine neo-baroque opulence with a modern functionalism. One of the central courtyards has also been radically changed by the addition of a glass roof and in its function as a lounge area is now an integral part of the Hotel. A vinotheque and rustic beer hall are now located next to the new wine cellar, with its groin vault, palisander wood furniture and marble floor. The furniture's light-coloured leather and the bright shade of the carpets are complemented by the red, blue and champagne colours in the suites. The basic hue predominating on any given storey appears as a small area of the floor and as the upholstery of the chairs and the beds' headboards. The teak of the parquet floors gives way to the bathrooms' stone flooring with its polished stainless steel inlays. Walls and fixtures of palisander wood and partially glazed walls add to the spa character of the bathrooms. As a nice touch all suites feature a glass methane gas fireplace.

above:
Presidential suite
conference / working area
mid:
Presidential suite
living /dining area

below:
Presidential suite
sleeping area

above left:
Presidential suite bathroom
above right:
Presidential suite additional
double bedroom
below:
Ground plans
1st and 3rd floor suites

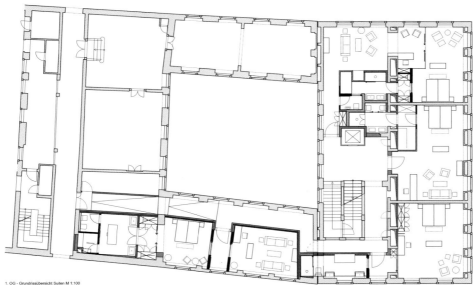

1. OG - Grundrissübersicht Suiten M 1:100

3. OG - Grundrissübersicht Suiten M 1:100

above:
Junior suite on 1st floor
mid:
Sleeping area 3rd floor suite

below:
Living / dining area
3rd floor suite

above and mid:
Double bed-rooms
on the 4th floor
below:
Living room 1st floor suite

Architecture:
Peter Straka,
Bernhard Edelmüller
Interior Design:
Michael Stelea
(4. / 5. floor)

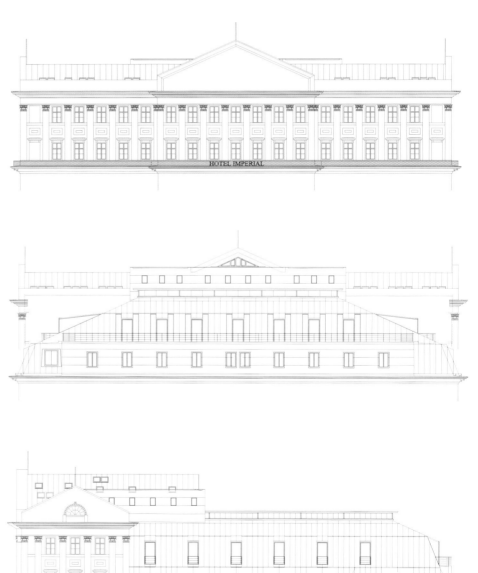

above:
Exterior view
below:
Sections
right:
Royal staircase

148

Vienna
Hotel Imperial

What began in 1863 as the private seat of the Prince of Württemburg became, on the occasion of the World Fair in 1873, the Hotel Imperial, an establishment synonymous with luxury. Located in the middle of Vienna, this former palace was an institution from the day of its opening onwards and it is not only the café of the same name that plays host to many celebrities from the world of politics and the arts. The Hotel is a shimmering showcase of 19th century chic. Stucco ceilings, breathtaking chandeliers, original furniture of the time, precious paintings and marble baths all testify to the Hotel's luxury and elegance. Following a period of major renovation and extensions new rooms and suites were created on the 4th and 5th floors providing guests with untrammelled views over the rooves of Vienna. The refined design and high standards of comfort give the ochre and yellow maisonette suites the character of penthouses. The Hotel's other rooms are also being brought up to the same pitch of excellence, with the curtains and silk awnings and covers in the rooms and suites on the Bel Etage floor being renewed and old furniture restored. The hall area has also received a face-lift based on historical records of what the interior once looked like.

left:
Salons

above right:
Grand festival hall
below right:
Ground plan

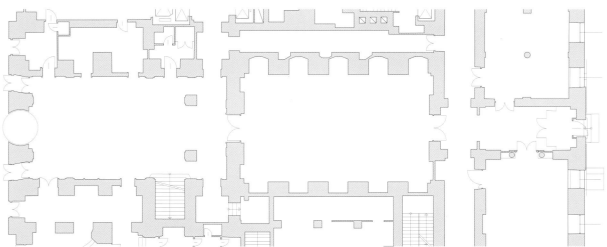

above:
Deluxe room
mid:
Executive junior suite

below:
Imperial Suite

above:
Royal Suite
below left:
Ground plan of suites
below right:
Cross sections

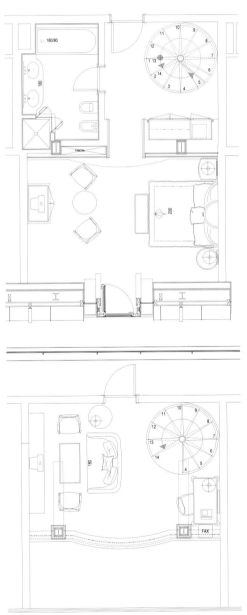

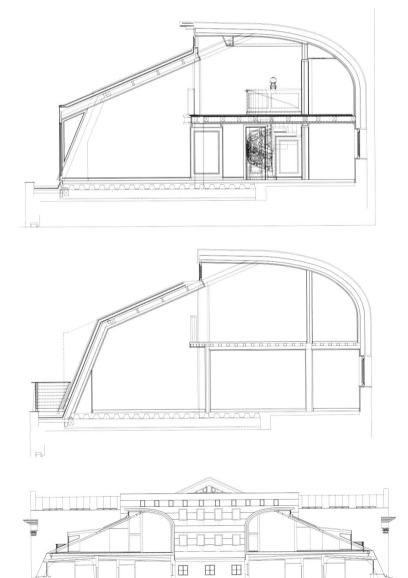

Interior Design:
Carlo Rampazzi

above:
Barbeque restaurant with
terrace on lake shore
below:
Drawing of entrance hall
right:
Hotel, view from the
swimming pool

154

Ascona
Hotel Eden Roc

Nestling on the shores of Lago Maggiore in a quiet, leafy area of Ascona, the Eden Roc Hotel exudes the aura of a Mediterranean palace. Interior architect Carlo Rampazzi has taken the romantic setting and produced a stylish, top-flight hotel that meets the desires and expectations of guests. Its charm can be attributed in large part to the array of warm colours and to the furniture designed specially by Rampazzi for the Hotel. The courtyard made of tiles with its murals are reminiscent of a small Italian mansion. The lakeshore restaurant, too, conjures up a concierge's lodge from a former age. Reception area, function rooms and dining rooms on the ground floor all have their individual character without clashing with the rest of the ensemble. The influence of Far Eastern philosophy is apparent in the architect's design of rooms and suites. Gentle angles, smooth surfaces and simple lines and a refined colour scheme are all instrumental in creating a balanced mood.

above left:
Restaurant "La Brezza"
above right:
Perspective of bar

below left:
Hall
below right (f.l.t.r.):
Chair, courtyard, bar

above:
Guest room
below:
Suite A

above left:
Suite B
above right:
Guest room
below:
Suite A

Architecture:
Marc Saugey (1950) |
Jean-Louis Christen
(refurbishment 1993)
Interior Design:
Chhada, Siembieda
& Partners |
Jean-Louis Christen

above:
Dining room
below:
Exterior view

160

Geneva

Mandarin Oriental Hotel du Rhône

The Mandarin Oriental Hotel du Rhône was built in 1950 in the heart of Geneva directly

adjacent to the swiftly flowing Rhône river. The noble early Art Deco style of the original building with its characteristic symmetrical elements and smooth curves was emphasised in the major refurbishment and conversion measures. Sunny, light, and warm colours create a soft, comfortable atmosphere. Italian marble, augmented by hand-woven rugs in the foyer, and parquet wooden flooring were used in all public spaces. The bathrooms of the rooms and suites are clad in elegant St. Helens marble from Greece. Precious materials such as leather, silk, and angora wool were used on the furniture that was completely fabricated in Switzerland. The 168 rooms and 22 suites are housed on seven floors. The Presidential Suite is located on the sixth floor with views out over the old city center, the river, and Lake Geneva. The upper level houses the Mont Blanc Suite named after the view of that mountain and the majestic Alpine scenery that the suite offers. This entire level offers splendid panorama views in all directions.

above:
Private dining

below:
Terrace of café Rafaei

above:
Special events in the hotels
private dining room
below:
The hotel's gastronomic
restaurant Le Neptune

above:
Deluxe suite bedroom
below:
All bathrooms with
St. Helens marble

above left and right:
The Mont Blanc Suite
below:
Mandarin terrace suite

Architecture:
Behles + Partners
Architects
(1992–2003), Zurich |
Ernst Anderegg,
Meiringen (1992)
Interior Design:
Jo Brinkmann,
Zurich (1992)

above:
Terrace with view on
Jungfernmassiv
below:
Front view
right:
Le Salle de Versailles

166

Interlaken

Victoria-Jungfrau Grand Hotel & Spa

Located across the triple-face of the Eiger, Mönch, and Jungfrau mountains in the

Bernese Oberland, the Jungfrau Hotel was built in 1869 by the architect Horace Edouard Davinet. Four years earlier he completed the neighbouring Victoria Hotel together with Friedrich Studer. In 1899, a joint stock company acquired the complex and constructed a central, domed building. The luxury hotel, located in the midst of the Interlaken spa health resort not far for Lake Brienz and Lake Thun soon advanced to an important destination for the powerful of the era. The imposing building was renovated in the early 1990's. In 1992, the Victoria Jungfrau Spa opened. A year later it was extended with the ESPA Wellness complex. In the high spa lobby teak furniture with beige-coloured cushions, and warmth-emanating dark orange and coal grey walls welcome guests. The imposing ceremonial halls "La Salle de Versailles" and "Le Salon Napoléon" are certainly the most powerful built expression of the establishment's 140-year history. Crystal chandeliers, high walls decorated with plaster and gold, and the coffered ceilings altogether convey the grand elegant atmosphere of the Belle Epoque era.

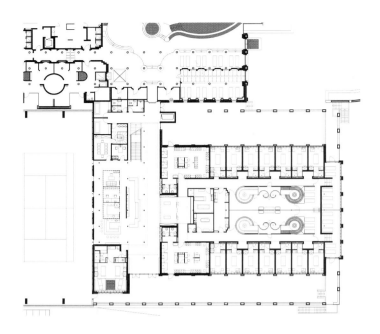

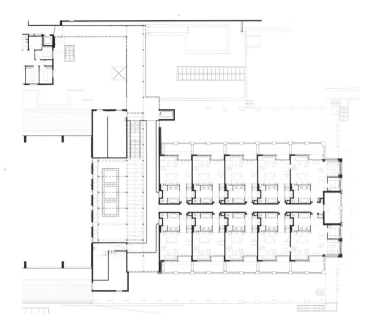

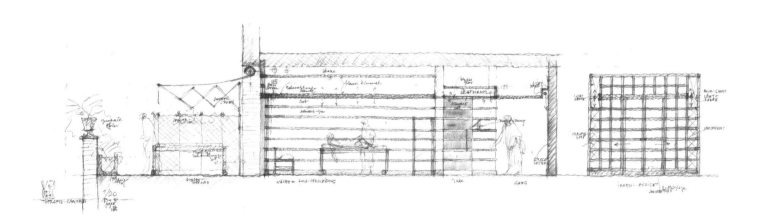

above left:
Ground plan ESPA area
above right:
Ground plan Belair suites
mid:
Cross section of
treatment room
below:
Treatment room

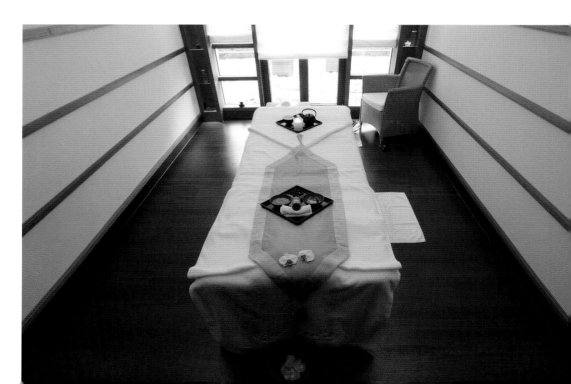

above:
ESPA entrance with shop
mid:
Private spa in ESPA

below left:
Steam bath
below right:
Swimming pool

above:
Junior suite
below right and left:
Duplex suite

above and mid:
Belair suite

below:
Double bedroom

Conversion:
Group l'Arche Sàrl
Architecture and
Planning – Bioret,
Sandoz, R. Estève
Architects
**Interior Design
Diskotheque, Bar,
Restaurant:**
Village Interior Design
– Alexandra de Garidel

above:
South facade
below:
Rotunda
right:
Bar

172

Lausanne

Lausanne Palace & Spa

The main building of the Lausanne Palace & Spa complex with its Neo-Baroque facade was completed in the heart of Lausanne in 1915. The hotel's 154 rooms and 30 suites with views of Lake Geneva and the Lausanne Cathedral are decorated in a range of styles including Empire, Louis-XVI and elegant Modernism. Exclusive textiles and harmonious colours imbue the spaces with an appropriate sense of restraint. The "Côté Jardin" restaurant also profits from the wonderful views, the terrace here offers a panorama of the lake. In the prize-crowned "Table d'Edgard" restaurant the Baroque furnishings are complemented with heavy curtains, gold and silver decorations, and velvet wall paper. Other facilities include the Cuban-style Bar du Palace with leather armchairs and wood panelling, and the LP's bar with modern interiors that invite one to enjoy some champagne. The Red Bar is an exclusive club open to club visitors and hotel guests. The CBE Concept Spa offers 2,100 m^2 of modern wellness facilities. A sparkling dais hovers above the pool next to imitations of classical frescoes on the walls.

173

left:
Restaurant
above:
La Rotunde
mid:
Restaurant

below:
Restaurant

above:
Junior suite with
view of the lake
below:
Swimming pool

above:
Guest room
below:
Suite

Interior Design:
Jean-Jaques Morrier
Interior Design Spa:
Jean-Jaques Morrier |
Alan Wanzenberg

above:
View from above
below:
Exterior view
right:
View of Lake Geneva
and the Alps

Vevey
Hôtel des Trois Couronnes

The Hotel Trois Couronnes (three crowns), built in 1842 in central Vevey between

Montreux and Lausanne, lies directly on the banks of Lake Geneva. The hotel has been home to numerous celebrities who valued Vevey's pleasant climate. The perhaps best known guest of the small town was Jean Jacques Rousseau. The Trois Couronnes has always been successful in entwining the history of the town with its own tradition. During the recent renovations, a successful mix of contrasting Belle Epoque and contemporary stylistic elements was achieved to create a modern first-class hotel. This mix of styles is especially evident in the rooms. Here the clear austerity of noble textiles is paired with works of Modern art, Napoleonesque dark-wooden nobility, and gentle beige tones. The two-storey central hall space with its marble columns underscores the sense of grand history prevalent throughout the establishment. Both the winter garden of the white-panelled Louis XV restaurant and the adjoining terrace offer unimpeded views of Lake Geneva.

above left:
Hallway

below:
Restaurant
right:
Lobby

above and below:
Room

above:
Way to swimming pool
mid:
Details of beauty salon

below:
Swimming pool in
Puressens Spa

wellness

islands

Architecture and
Interior Design:
Flum Design

above:
Exterior view
below:
Entrance

Rostock-Warnemünde

This hotel complex, which opened in 2005, enjoys a majestic location directly on

Yachthafenresidenz Hohe Düne

the Baltic coast. To the west, the guests have a commanding view of the *Neuer Strom* shipping channel, to the north they look out over the open sea, and to the east there's the *Hohe Düne* yachting marina. Thanks to its unaffected Mediterranean-inspired architecture, the building complex effortlessly blends into its spacious, park-like surroundings. The Residence's light-colored façade contrasts with its dark-brown mahogany windows and doors and many fine copper details. This compound of warm tones and natural materials continues in the interior. The lobby, which is furnished with fine hardwoods and fitted with a rustic fireplace, emphasizes the maritime ambience. In creating the 368 rooms and suites, each with a spacious marble bathroom, the hotel's designers placed particular emphasis on details in brass and mahogany. The wellness area, spread over 4,200 m², offers three separate spa zones: in addition to the understatedly designed Oasis of Stillness and rooms offering traditional spa treatments, there is a newly-opened section designed in the style of a luxury yacht. This boasts a 22 x 10 meters panorama swimming pool with a separated lounge area and open fireplace.

left:
Fireplace
above:
Room

mid:
Bathroom
below:
Detail bathroom

above:
Detail wellness area
right:
Wellness area

mid:
Swimming pool with
open fireplace
below:
View of the *Neuer Strom*

Architecture:
Sigrid Bock
Interior Design:
Family Clausing

above:
View of the farmers garden
below:
Countryside spa with
outdoor pool

192

Burg im Spreewald
Zur Bleiche Resort & Spa

The Zur Bleiche Resort & Spa is located in the marvellous Spreewald landscape on a site where army uniforms for Frederick the Great's army were once bleached. The Clausing family bought the buildings located on a 26,000 m² site in 1992. The hotel was extended in several building phases and the free-standing buildings were interconnected. Wood exterior sheathing was foreseen to embed the buildings in the surrounding context. A major developmental impulse occurred in 1998 when the 2,000 m² Landtherme thermal bath complex was completed. In 2003, after a fire, it was completed and extended with a 25 m outdoor swimming pool. The materials used in the wellness facilities are all historically typical in the region: natural woods, linen, and natural white chalk rendering all contribute to creating generous, pleasant spaces that make good use of the large available site. The hotel's unobtrusive country house style with warm coloured terracotta tiles and wooden floors is additionally underscored by select, carefully placed antiques and objects of art.

above and mid:
Restaurant Biosphäre
above right:
In the lobby

below left:
Lobby
below right:
Site plan

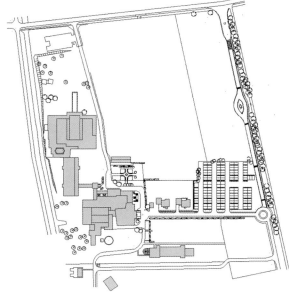

above:
Countryside spa,
indoor pool with fireplace
below:
Ground plan spa

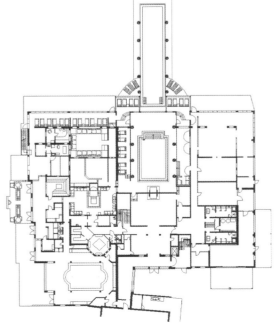

above and below:
Countryside spa
wellness area

Architecture and
Interior Design:
Flum Design

above:
Exterior view
below:
Ground plan of
wellness area
right:
Steam bath

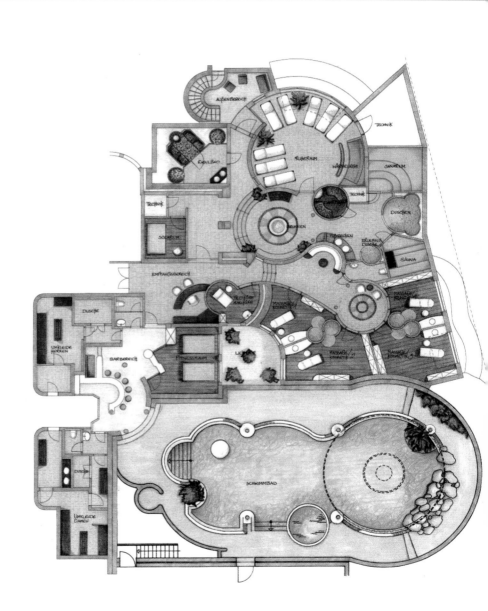

198

Rotenburg
Hotel Landhaus Wachtelhof

The Landhaus Wachtelhof is located in an idyllic forest in Rotenburg an der Wümme,

between Bremen, Hamburg, and Hanover. The surrounding nature reserve extends right up to the park-like hotel grounds with their old stands of trees. The remote hotel buildings create a gentle transition to the surrounding gardens and relay a sense of security and safety that is underscored by quaint towers, curving balconies and the low-drawn roof that encloses the rooms and suites. The glazed conservatory on the garden side allows the surrounding natural landscape to flow into the complex. A low-key, luxurious, friendly atmosphere is achieved inside through use of wood, gentle forms, and subtle colours. Solely natural and exclusive materials including stone, wood, cotton, and wool were used inside the hotel rooms and suites. All 38 rooms and suites are individually decorated. The Mediterranean "Wachtelhof-Therme" thermal baths provide guests with extensive wellness facilities in the tradition of ancient Roman bathing culture.

above:
Reception
mid:
Room
above right:
Main entrance of
restaurant l' Auberge

below left:
Entrance
below right:
Room

above and mid:
Cosmetic waiting areas
above right:
Cleopatra cave

below left:
Resting area
below right:
Warmth bed in resting area
and shower

Architecture:
Friedensreich
Hundertwasser

above:
Art house
below:
Green roofs of the quarters

Bad Blumau

This unique thermal bath facility is effectively embedded in the landscape of Austria's

Rogner Bad Blumau Hotel & Spa

southern Styria hills. None other than the renown Austrian artist Friedensreich Hundertwasser (1928–2000) designed and built it in collaboration with the owner Robert Rogner. The formative design principle was to create a hotel landscape of built fields and hills as an evocative statement contrasting typical the typical concrete, glass, and steel of so many modern-day hotels. Hundertwasser's philosophy of living in harmony with nature found expression in the thermal bath facility. The baths are fed with water from the Melchior spring and encompass 2,724 m^2 of interior and exterior water surfaces, a fresh-water wellness pool, and a sauna landscape with a rock sauna. Keeping in accordance with Hundertwasser's notion that every human being has the right to a window each building wing, and each window is different. Curving forms, golden domes, and a rich range of colours – typical elements in Hundertwasser designs – combine to make the Rogner-Bad Blumau the largest of his inhabitable artworks.

left:
Tree of life
above:
Health center
"FindYourself"
mid:
The golden dome of the
main building

below:
2,400 different windows

above:
Sunrise at Hundertwasser's
mid:
The art of Vulkania
right:
Hundertwasserpillars

below:
Indoor thermae

Architecture and Interior Design
Wellness Area:
Wolfgang Pöschl
Interior Design Old Building:
Kay Sperling

above:
Exterior view
below:
Deck-chairs to relax
right:
Archaic decoration
with tea bar

210

Kitzbühel
Schwarzer Adler

The Schwarzer Adler in Kitzbühel – known far and wide for the cuisine of its

Neuwirt Restaurant – has succeeded in establishing itself in recent years as one of the most popular wellness addresses around. Its rustic character asserts itself fully in the rooms, more subtly in the open-fire room in the reception area. The new wellness area has been designed along the Hotel's traditional Tirol architecture lines and is a perfect example of the skilful combination of old and new. Fitness area, sauna and pool each occupy a different level. Large expanses of glass exploit daylight to the full and throw the Hotel into exciting relief at night. Daylight is even channelled down as far as the sauna area in the basement. Smooth walls and the clear formal language used in the architecture are not intrusive and allow guests the space to unwind. The indoor pool, bordered on one of its short sides by an exposed concrete wall, is inclined towards the street with its glass ceiling half-open yet with swimmers nonetheless shielded from prying eyes. The fitness room above is of such sweeping dimensions that free rein can be given to the gaze.

left:
Hotel lobby with open
fireplace and bar
mid:
Restaurant
above right:
Wellness area

below left:
View from the tea bar
towards the indoor pool
below right:
Ground plans
1st and 2nd basement

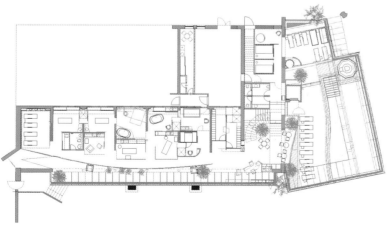

above:
Junior suite
mid:
Room Walde

below:
Suite designed by
Wolfgang Pöschl

above:
Entrance to the pool and
the panorama fitness center
mid:
Detail fresh air-room:
the three components
wood, concrete and stone
below:
Meditation room with
waterbeds and fire

Architecture:
Patrice Reynaud
Interior Design:
Jacques Garcia

above:
Exterior view
below:
La Réserve - boat
right:
Entrance and lobby

216

Geneva
La Réserve Hotel & Spa

The Hotel La Réserve, located in four hectares of parkland beside Lake Geneva, offers guests all the comforts associated with 85 rooms and 17 suites, most of them boasting their own patio or balcony, two restaurants, each including a bar and lounge, and a 2,000 m² spa area. The French star architect Jacques Garcia has created stylishly furnished interiors featuring colour schemes ranging from savannah to rainforest. A recurrent theme are the lamps and lights decorated with bird sculptures. Parquet floors and suede-lined bedclothes are juxtaposed with embroidered wallpaper in the rooms and suites. In the bathrooms gleaming marble mosaics compete with sleek, black granite and appliqués of mahogany and steel. The huge spa area offers 17 massage and treatment rooms and indoor and outdoor pools. Dark rattan loungers with elegant, white padding are arranged in front of jellyfish-shaped lamps and windows and walls draped in material. Passing through the areas connecting different sections of the Une Autre Histoire Restaurant guests may relax in chairs upholstered in white leather.

217

left and below:
Tsé fung restaurant
above:
Library and restaurant Loti

above left:
Indoor spa pool
above right:
Suite La Réserve

below left:
Bar and restaurant at spa
and detail spa
below right:
Deluxe room

**Project Management,
Refurbishment,
Interior Design:**
Jaggi & Partners
**Architecture
New Building:**
Tschanz Architecture
Interior Design:
Raumforum
Balmer and Krieg
**Construction
Implementation:**
FSW Architecture

above and below:
Exterior view

Lenk im Simmental
Lenkerhof Alpine Resort

The Lenkerhof has seen many periods of structural modification and expansion. The most recent project for drastic redesign put an end to the random juxtaposition of many of the building's elements and instead created a sequential arrangement of staff building, hotel and wellness area on the sloping topography in such a way that a small, private park with outdoor pool came into being. At the same time the old facade of the Hotel was given fresh materials and new colours and the ground floor winter garden was extended. The interior design is striking in style and has been executed with guests in mind. Individual elements such as the hatched branches construction in the hall serve as an emphatic framework for any occasion. Velvet-upholstered chairs, the large fireplace surrounded by its wall of books and the slightly secluded bar are all conducive to rest and recuperation. Just as the resort has a wide range of activities and services on offer so the adventurous spirit of the wellness area's architecture is nourished on the most powerful of alpine sulphur sources and the purest of natural elements. Intense red and blue surfaces on the interior symbolize fire and the omnipresent water. The indoor pool area and the glass walkway to the outdoor pool allow spectacular views of the mountain scenery.

above:
Outdoor pool
below:
Igloo

above:
Winter garden
below:
Pavilion

above:
Beauty reception
mid:
Crystal tub
above right:
Guest room

below left:
Steam bath
below right:
Southern facade

Architecture:
Peter Zumthor

above:
Exterior view
right:
Resting area in
indoor swimming pool

Vals
Therme Vals

The sedate mountain village Vals lies at the end of Vals Valley at the base of 3,000

meter-high mountains. Natural wells made the remote place a health destination. Since 1996, Peter Zumthor's unusual architecture has attracted additional visitors. The rectangular solitary building with its green roof is half embedded in the mountainside and half opens toward the light via large glazed surfaces on the valley side. Walls constructed of horizontally laid natural stone slabs define spatial boundaries. The massive, slate-like texture of the Vals Gneis stone plates quarried from the nearby quarry plays a major role in defining the unique atmosphere. Quartz layers ranging in colour from green to blue alternate with light grey to white layers. A striking precision of design unites all of the layered surfaces: floors, ceilings, stairs, and stone benches. A subterranean connecting corridor leads to the hotel. Eleven rooms here were also designed by Peter Zumthor, and more will follow. White-painted cement floors, blue-black rugs, Thai silk curtains, and linen sheets characterise their design.

above:
The thermae
below:
Indoor pool

above and below:
Indoor pool

above and below:
Rooms in the main building

urban

hideouts

Architecture:
Architecture Practice
Prof. Manfred
Schomers and
Rainer Schürmann,
Bremen
Design Concept:
Rahe + Rahe Design,
Bremen
**Planning and
Implementation:**
Tombusch &
Brumann

above:
Exterior facade
below:
Generous lobby for
receiving the guests

236

Bremen
Atlantic Hotel Galopprennbahn

The new Atlantic Hotel adjacent to the race course opened its doors to the public on 1st July 2005. The light, modern interior architecture reflects a creativity that is at once unostentatious and inspiring. The design favours clear and concise colours and uses motifs from nature and the world of horse racing. Guests are able to observe the action on the race course through the glass rear of the building. The hotel's interior alludes both visually and thematically to the equestrian location. Conspicuous here is the grass green of a reception desk in the form of stylised hedges in front of a photo of a race situation. The two-storey-high hotel lobby area, with a gallery on the first floor leading to conference rooms, bar and restaurant, gives an immediate impression of space. As an alternative to the social environment of the bar the restaurant also offers more secluded seating towards the rear. The colour scheme and motifs are continued throughout the 116 rooms and suites that make up the three floors of the hotel.

above and below:
The guests participate of the actions on the hippodrome trough the windows streching from the floor to the ceiling
mid:
Horse racing is the central theme in the entire hotel

above right:
Restaurant
below right:
Bar

Ansicht A

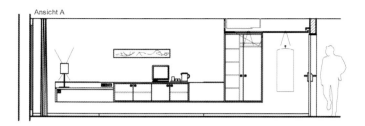

Ansicht B

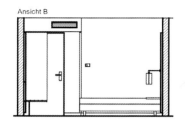

Ansicht D

Grundriss

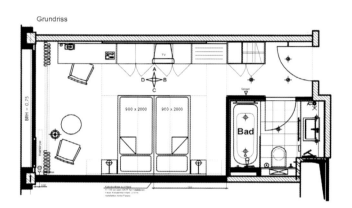

Ansicht C (Variante 1)

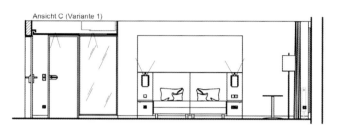

Ansicht C (Variante 2)

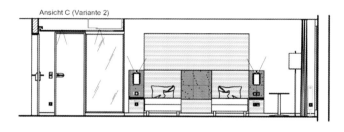

above:
Views and ground plan
below:
The arrangement of the
different coloured tiles
characterises the bathroom

above and below:
Orange and brown are the
dominating colours in the
rooms

Architecture:
RKW Rhode
Kellermann
Wawrowsky,
Düsseldorf
Interior Design:
Bernd Elfers

above:
Hotel hall / reception
below:
Entrance with floating
roof canvas
above right:
Lifts
below right:
Restaurants

Bremen
Inn Side Premium Hotel

This hotel is located on the banks of the Weser river just steps away from Europe's

largest indoor theme park, the Bremen Space Park. The architecture of the four-storey hotel complex furthers the futuristic theme set by the Space Park. A 400 m² central hall space forms the heart of the four star hotel. The minimalist design scheme is underscored by smooth modern surfaces in blue, mint, yellow, and black. LED lighting allows the reception desk to seem to hover above the floor. A design focus within the space is formed by the aluminium and glass Skywalker Bar. Sails hung from the ceiling are illuminated in various colours by fibre-optics to create a futuristic atmosphere. The wall surfaces of the river-fronting restaurant are clad with matte metal panels. In addition to the Galaxis conference facilities with three multi-functional meeting halls, wellness and fitness facilities round off the array of uses incorporated into the hotel complex. A half-glazed lift that allows views into the black-lit lift shaft transports guests to the studios, suites, and family rooms.

above left:
Bar, illuminated glass
above right:
Bar roof canvas, LED light

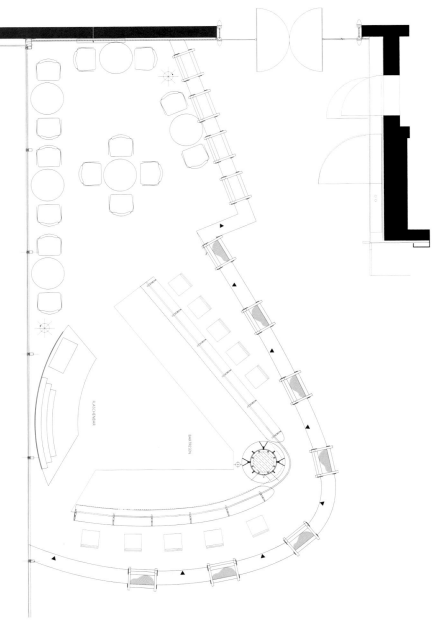

below left:
Ground plan bar and chairs
below right:
Ground floor plan

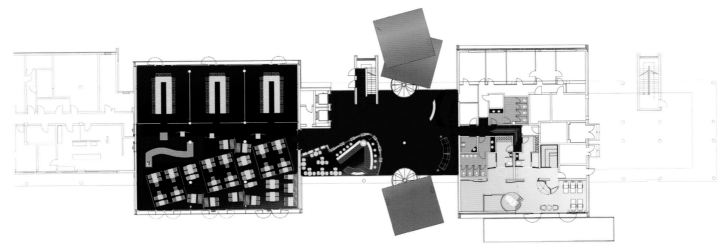

above:
Glass bathroom

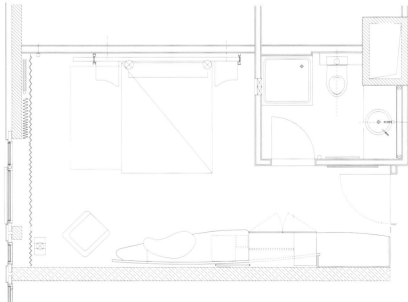

below:
Ground plan room

above:
Hotel room
mid:
Hotel room
¨glass bathroom¨
below:
Wellness resting area

Architecture:
Architecture Practice
Oana Rosen

above:
Garden
below:
Exterior view
right:
Reception

Frankfurt
Bristol Hotel

Following a change of ownership the decision came in 2003 to remodel the Bristol

Hotel. The result was a design hotel and event venue that far exceeded the traditional notion of a hotel's function. Day and night, winter and summer, the establishment is now a warm and inviting modern oasis. The open-plan lobby, reception area and 24-hour bar form the introduction to the hotel. A dark, smoked-oak parquet floor, beige leather, wenge-coloured furniture and pleated lighting ensure an atmospheric warmth. Ultra modern touches are provided by such elements as the broad, rear-lit, multicoloured curtains and the dark red, decorative cubes on the wall of the passage linking lobby and function rooms, cubes that can be decorated to fit season and event. The huge mirror in the lobby is balanced by the Bristol Summer Lounge, a garden oriental in character possessing ponds, foliage-decked walls and dark wooden floorboards. Universally deployable furniture elements were specially designed for the 145 rooms, which also adopted the materials used in the communal areas.

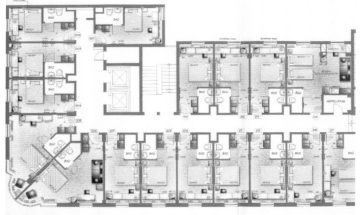

above:
Reception
below:
Layout plan

above:
Breakfast area
below:
Bristol Bar

above:
Room

below:
Room

above:
Hall
below:
Room

Architecture:
John Seifert
Architects
Interior Design:
Adam Tihany
(public areas) |
Matteo Thun (rooms,
conference and
wellness area)
Project Development:
HOCHTIEF Projekt-
entwicklung GmbH,
Rhein-Main

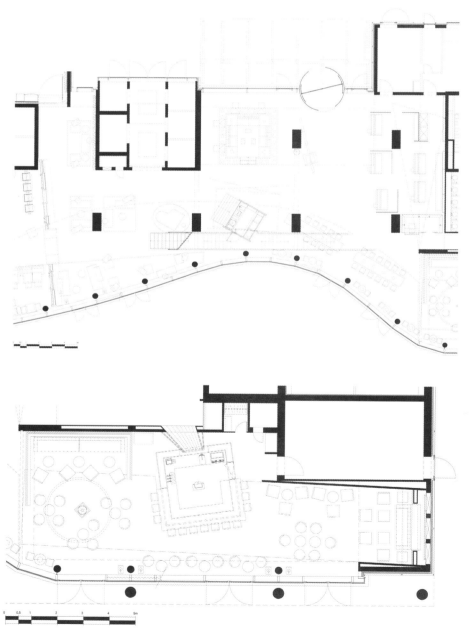

above:
View from southwest
below:
Ground plan
lobby and cigar bar
right:
View from Opel-Rondell

Frankfurt
Radisson SAS Hotel

Frankfurt's skyline is now enriched by a new 20-storey, 96 meter high edifice. The striking business hotel lures customers with an enticing steel and glass structure that forms a blue, light-reflecting vertical slab. The new building designed by renown architects as a flagship of the Radisson fleet is characterised by a minimalist, modern – and thanks to the openness of the rooms on all exterior sides – light-filled design. A six meter high, hovering tower containing 1,500 bottles of wine creates a special accent in the lobby. The reception area with its accompanying counter satellites is also welcoming and light-filled. The ambience inside the hotel rooms is heightened by excellent views of the skyline and the Taunus mountains. Four room categories are distributed throughout the tower floors. The "at home" rooms located on the second to fifth floors are decorated with warm, yet modern elements. Comfortable understatement interiors are deployed in the next levels, and intensive colours were used in the rooms above the tenth floor. The wellness facilities are located in a 500 m² large space on the 18th floor and – thanks to the expansive glazing – command breathtaking views.

above:
"At home" (2nd–5th floor)
below:
"At home" – classic,
welcoming, warm

above:
"Chic", wireless lan
in entire hotel
below:
"Chic" (6th–9th floor) –
without time,
understatement, pleasure

above:
"Fashion" (10th–13th floor)
below:
"Fashion" – vibrating,
colourful, cosy

above and mid:
"Fresh" (14th–17th floor) –
glamour, daring, surprising
below:
"Fresh", free broadband
service and flat screens in
entire hotel

Architecture:
Kajima Corp. Japan
Interior Design:
Bost Berlin
Interior Design
Architecture

above:
Restaurant "Falco"
below:
View of hall

260

Leipzig
The Westin Leipzig

The 27-floor 5-star hotel near the city center was originally a gift from Japan to the former GDR. The modern interior design of the top floor is Asian in flavour. Overhead illuminations in fluid colour designs greet guests as they approach the lift. Bar and lounge have been created around a bar covered in Makassa wood panelling. A highlight of the restaurant is its walk-in red wine storeroom built of glass and maintained at a steady room temperature. The board rooms feature flat-screen monitors which are built into the wall and integrate well with the rest of the rooms' fittings. Glass doors sporting abstract motifs from Japanese stone art open into the washrooms. The siting of the suites at the corner of the hotel gives guests a magnificent view over the city in two directions. All lights, furniture and carpets were designed and produced exclusively for the suites of the Leipzig Westin. In their form, colour and ornamentation they have a timeless beauty and exude relaxation and elegance.

above:
View of bar
mid:
Boardroom

below:
Toilet installation

above:
Ground plan of 27th floor

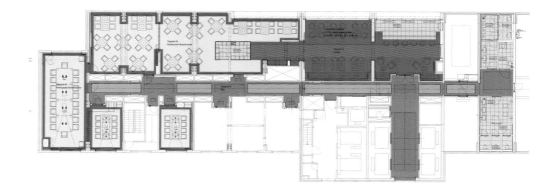

below:
Lift foyer

above:
Bedroom corner suite
mid:
Bathroom corner suite

below:
Ground plan corner suite

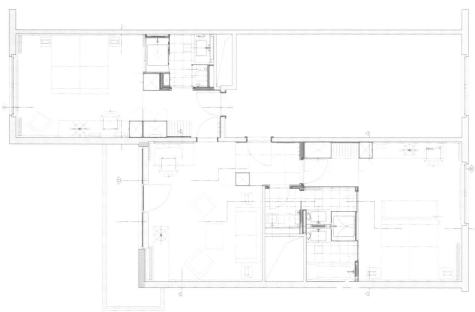

above:
Bedroom corner suite
below:
Living room corner suite

Architecture:
Tony Schmidbauer
Interior Design:
Bost Berlin
Interior Design
Architecture

above, below and right:
Detailed views of suite

266

Munich

ArabellaSheraton Bogenhausen

The Arabella Sheraton Bogenhausen has its roots in a 1969 boarding house designed by

architect Tony Schmidbauer. The 'urban block-within-a-building' design grew out of Le Corbusier's idea of an 'Unité d'habitation' providing residential units, workplaces, retail outlets and leisure facilities under a single roof. As well as the standard flats for rent the building also contains hotel rooms. The prize-winning concept links up room, bathroom and entrance via glazed panels in the walls. The practical, multi-use curtains can transform the open-plan layout into discrete séparées with a silent sweep of fabric. The ergonomically designed workplace has been conceived with meticulous attention to detail and offers all state-of-the-art communications technology. The hotel rooms, with their gentle colour schemes, are intended as places of peace and quiet. The gleaming dark brown of the Makassa wood surfaces contrast with bright creams and soft grey-browns. Both in the natural light of day and under the building's refined artificial lighting the interior design soothes and relaxes hotel guests.

above:
Double room
below:
Single room

268

above:
View of bathroom
below:
Ground plan of single and
double room

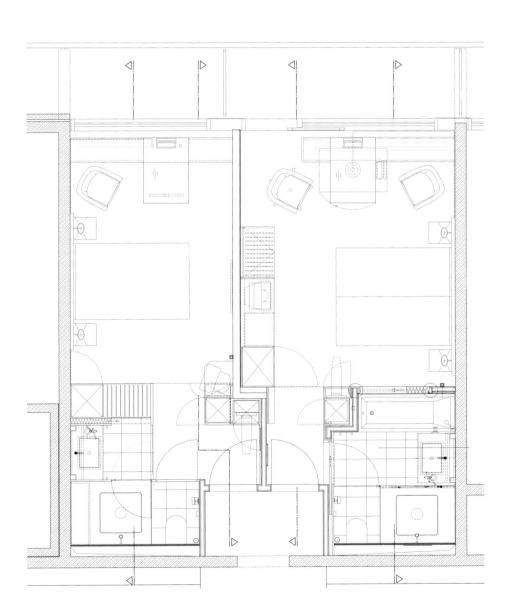

above:
Living / dining area of suite
below:
Detail double bedroom

270

above:
Detail of suite
below:
Ground plan of suite

Interior Design:
KSH
Hotelbetriebs GmbH,
Diana Bartl

above:
Entrance area with
fresh flowers
below:
Patio in front of
historic facade

272

Munich
Hotel Restaurant Ritzi

In 1997, the Ritzi restaurant was built in a 100 year old house that would soon be

renown in all of Munich. And the striking hotel also located here wouldn't remain a secret for long either. Before Ritzi moved in the building housed a theatre and an unspectacular restaurant. Now, the restaurant, bar, and lounge all present themselves in unified Art Déco Style. Walls panelled in noble light wood and Art-Déco lamps were installed in all public spaces. Red armchairs also found in Milan's Scala opera house create spatial accents in the lounge and emphasise the comfortable, friendly atmosphere. The hotel rooms were decorated to a contrasting array of differing themes: Chinese, Art Déco, African, Mexican, Indonesian and purely colourful motifs alternate in the rooms. Wall paintings, numerous small photographs mounted on the walls, sculptures on the cornices, and decorative elements such as surf boards or hammocks all contribute to creation of the unique hotel atmosphere.

273

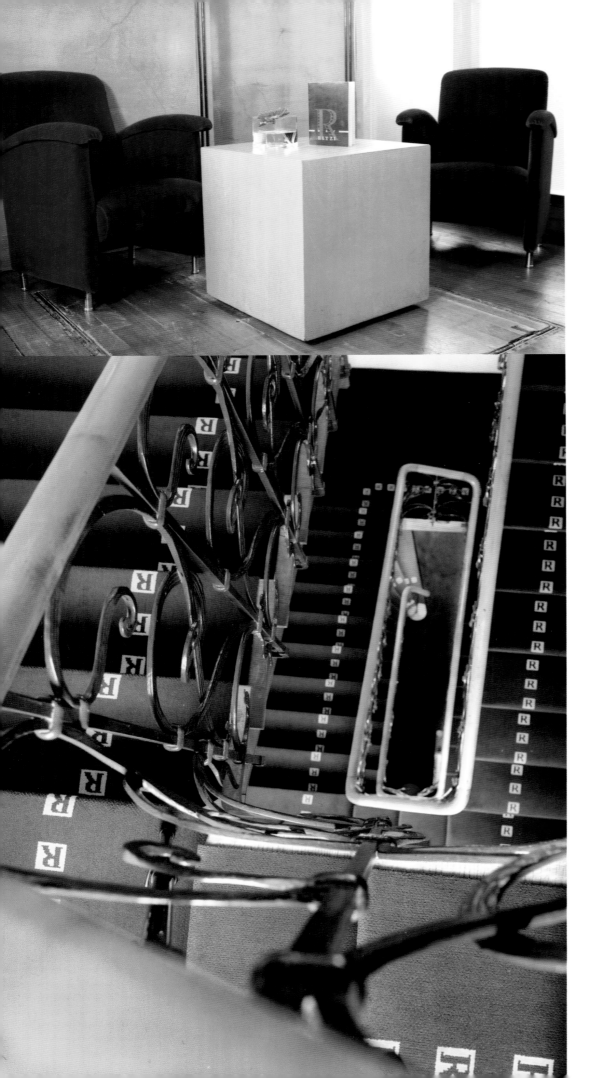

above:
Lounge
right:
Bar

below:
Staircase

above:
Room 26 "African room"
below:
Room 23 "Chinese room"

above:
Room 35 "Red room"
below:
Room 32 "Caribbean room"

**Architecture
and Design:**
Firm Hüttinger
Exhibition Engineering
and Claus Lämmle

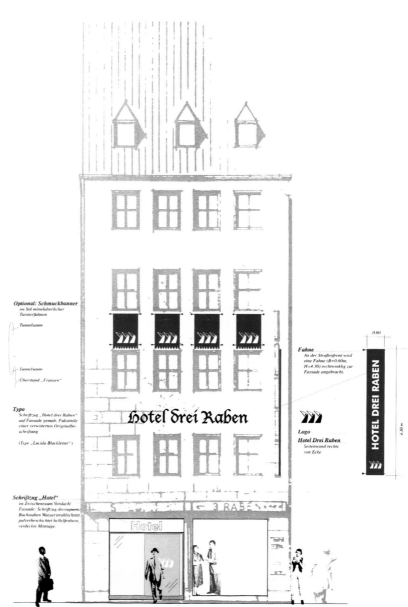

above:
Script and painting
at the wall
below:
Design of facade
right:
Lounge and bar

278

Nuremberg

Hotel Drei Raben

The three-raven shield has graced this house in Nuremberg's center for cen-

turies. Inside, these ravens tell different stories based on old Nuremberg myths in each of the 25 rooms. Sandstone reliefs, accessories, and artfully decorated texts on the walls all were implemented to relay the various myths. The multimedia presentation of a common theme throughout the entire design was emphasised in the lounge where the Nuremberg myths presented in the rooms are projected onto a ten-meter long textile curtain surface with video projectors. Other types of audio-visual presentations are also possible here. The lounge was conceived as a central space for communication accessible to both hotel guests and the public. The reception desk, a café bar for greeting drinks, breakfast area, and the hotel lobby are spatially and functionally integrated. Glaring red chairs originally seen in the film "2001: A Space Odyssey", design-classic swivel chairs, ivory-coloured flooring and noble curtains merge playfully to create a unique ambience of soft-forms.

above, mid and below:
Hotel lounge and cocktail
bar – through the use of
light in three different
colours

above:
Round bar counter with
taffeta curtain in the lobby
below:
Round reception counters
in the lobby

left:
Bed in the room of the local football team 1. FC Nuremberg with goal and goalkeeper made of sandstone

mid:
Sandstone relief, script and painting in the room "Deep Fountain"

below:
Kicker panelled with cherry tree wood in the room of 1. FC Nuremberg

Georg Kennemann

Ferdinand Wenauer

Norbert Eder

Horst Leupold

Max Morlock

left:
St. Lorenz church made of
sandstone in the room by
Peter Henlein
mid:
Toy room with paintings and
little sandstone towers
below:
Time machine by Peter
Henlein and the bathtub in
the ravon gabel

Architecture:
Thomas Rudolf
Interior Design:
Karen Heldmann

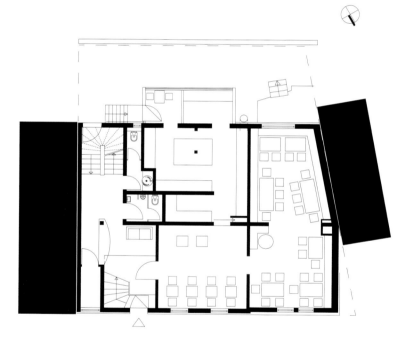

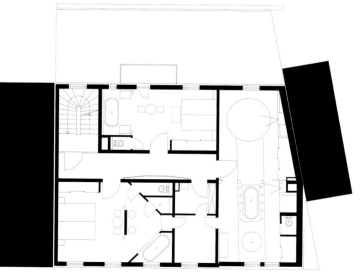

above:
Exterior view
below:
Ground plans ground floor
and 1st floor with rooms
"Titanic", "Hermitage" and
"Cloud No. 7"
right:
Lounge

284

Stuttgart
Zauberlehrling

The Heldmanns, operators of the Zauberlehrling Restaurant, have created a small and unique 9-room hotel close to the center of Stuttgart. Restoration work began in 2001 to dismantle the existing infrastructure of a building that had long since ceased to function as a hotel and strip it down to its skeleton. The water and air heating units were banished to the top of the building to make room for the restaurant operations. A flat roof was removed, making way for a terrace offering an attractive view over Stuttgart's Talkessel district. The fact that the doors are not numbered is testimony to the individual character of the rooms, whose one common feature is the open-plan bath. The "Mondschau" room, for instance, is slightly Asiatic in atmosphere and uses fine but minimalist materials such as Irish limestone and gold leaf wall finishes. The "Hermitage" is fitted out in the warm, red opulence of a French country house whilst the "Black Box" offers its occupants the more technical feel provided by slate, concrete and olive wood.

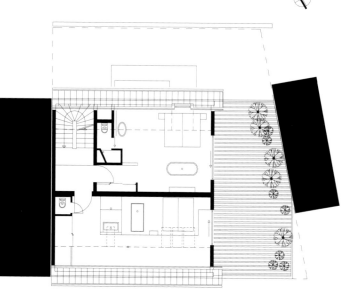

above:
Restaurant with
standig tables
below:
Ground plan top floor with
rooms ¨Paddington¨ and
¨Mondschau¨

above:
Bathroom "Black Box"
below:
Guest room "Cloud No. 7"

left:
"Paddington" ancient
copper tub in front of
open fireplace
above left:
Detail in room "Hermitage"
above right:
Room "Zeitfalle"
below:
Bathtub in room
„Mondschau"

countryside

hotels

Architecture:
Ralph Barenbrock |
HEP Simon,
Simon + Partners
Room Design:
Elvira Bach | Moritz
Götze | Gerd
Mackensen | Lale
Meer | Sibylle Prangel
Cornelia Schleime

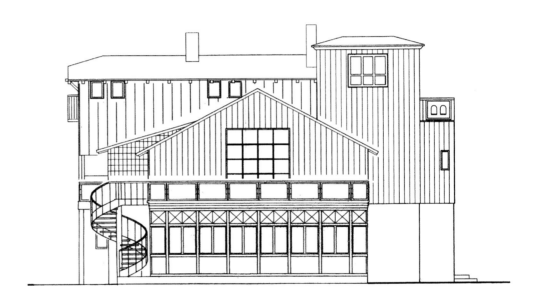

above:
View of the street
by night
below:
North-east and
south-west facade
right:
In front of the door

Ahrenshoop
Hotel Elisabeth von Eicken

The Elisabeth von Eicken brings together in one hotel all the trademark features of the former Ahrenshoop artists colony – extraordinary architecture, a unique gallery, a fine restaurant and hotel rooms that are artworks in their own right. A century ago the painter Elisabeth von Eicken (1862–1940) built her own home and studio here. In 1997 the dilapidated house was taken over by two architects and gallery owner Sabine Peters-Barenbrocks and transformed into a small hotel for individualists and art connoisseurs. Loving restoration and the various uses to which different parts of the building have been put have created a small hotel that combines traditional flavour and a charm that is all its own. The project to turn the building into a gallery / restaurant / hotel was completed in 1999. Paintings and sculptures are on display in the garden as well as in the building, with an outdoor sculpture by Berlin artist Hubertus von der Goltz creating an especially striking impression. The six individually furnished hotel rooms are the work of young artists of renown. The gallery on the first floor exhibits new art at regular intervals.

above:
Gallery
below:
Ground plan of ground floor

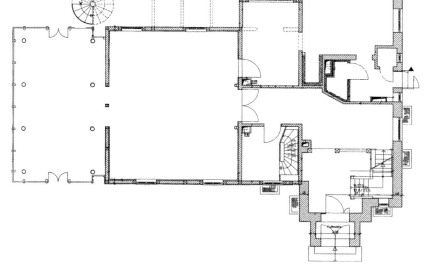

above and below:
Winter garden

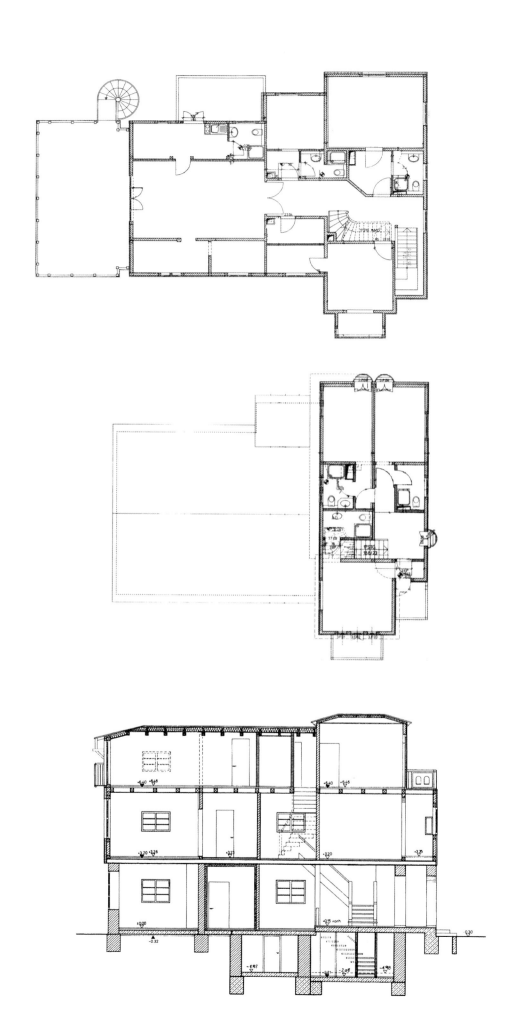

above:
Ground plan 1st floor
mid:
Ground plan top floor
below:
Cross section

296

above left:
Guest room "Sibylle Range"
above right:
Guest room "Elvira Bach"
below:
Staircase with historic tiles
and old stairs

Architecture:
Architecture Practice
Peter Weber, Cologne
Interior Design:
Planning Office Hüls,
Klemens Hüls

above:
On the dune, seaward
below:
Driveway to Söl'ring Hof
right:
Library

Sylt

Dorint Sofitel Söl'ring Hof Sylt

The Accor Group manages its remarkable hotel on Germany's best known North Sea island, in a secluded location that promises guests absolute peace and quiet. The old guest house of the Sylter Hof, but recently a run-down building, is now a gleaming white establishment with reet-thatched roof offering guests sweeping views of the sea and nature reserve from its position on the dunes. In designing the communal areas and the 15 individually laid-out rooms the interior designer has managed to avoid ostentatious luxury and modern austerity. The decision sprang from an understanding that the special character of the hotel's location could not and should not be subordinated to the whims of mere mortals. The result is an interior that has retained its own natural, benevolent character by means of a blend of fine materials. A number of interesting design details crop up throughout the hotel. The open-plan nature of the restaurant kitchen on the first floor is an echo of the colours and wide open spaces of the natural surroundings. Johannes King's French cuisine, with its dash of local maritime character, confers another vein of individualism on this little hotel.

above:
Ground plan and
views of fireplace

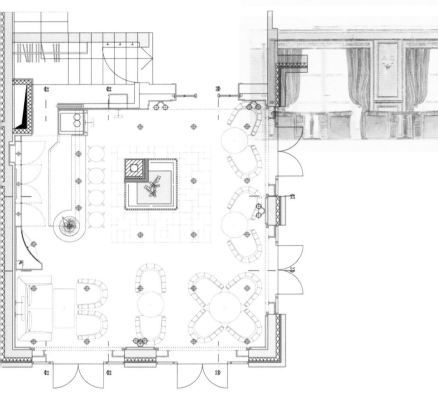

below left:
Fireplace
below right:
Library

above:
Restaurant views of
show kitchen
below:
Restaurant

left:
Guest room with sea view
above:
Guest room with fireplace

below left:
Maisonette guest room
below right:
Detail in guest room
bathroom

Architecture:
Architecture Practice
Werner Behrens
Interior Design:
Flum Design

above:
Gable, seen from garden
below:
Terraces of guest rooms

Sylt
Landhaus Stricker

The original reet-thatched-roof house built in 1784 was operated as a hotel even

before construction of a further building in typical country house style. The extension concept foresaw complete refurbishment and modernisation of the existing structure and rooms and wellness facilities in the new building. A new fireplace room was built in the entrance area of the original building. The existing restaurant was designed in typical country house style with black-painted wooden beams, Bordeaux-red walls, and white rendered, semicircular windows. The room interiors also place comfort in the forefront. Thick wool rugs of the highest-quality, and specially designed furniture with alternating cherry wood and creme-coloured lacquer were foreseen here. Noise-protection windows and a special ventilation system that allows for natural air circulation even when the windows are closed guarantee absolute tranquility. A combination of Italian and hand-painted Moroccan tiles were used in the bathrooms. The design of the wellness facilities continues this atmosphere with terracotta tiles and wall paintings.

above:
Restaurant Bodendorf
mid:
Fireplace in entrance area
above right:
Restaurant terrace

below left:
Library
below right:
View

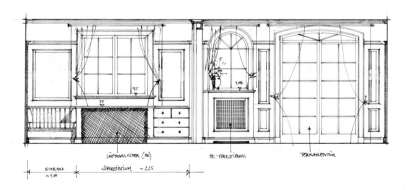

right and above:
Guest room
mid:
Ground plan of room

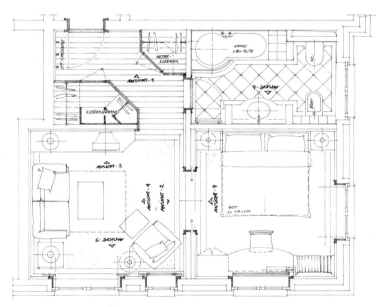

below:
Swimming pool

Architecture and
Interior Design:
pla.net
Landscaping:
Idealice –
techn. Büro für
Landschaftsplanung,
Alice Größinger

above:
Exterior view
below:
Ground plan ground floor
right:
Reception

Mayerling

Hanner Restaurant Hotel Meetingpoint

The Hanner Restaurant and Hotel Meetingpoint is a classic example of how a carefully

thought out concept and its single-minded execution can attract the buying public. The architects' task was to create the perfect working environment for star chef Heinz Hanner to produce his exclusive dishes. The result is an area crafted specifically in the interests of culinary excellence and reflective of the three-way dialogue between architecture, interior design and landscape design. The materials used represent the Austrian countryside of the Wienerwald. Large windows provide views of the garden and the surrounding natural features. Sandstone, slate, glass and larch and birch wood are all employed prominently in the interior of the hotel. The art works of the Jünger Gallery provide the decorative detail. The remodelling of the hotel was not restricted to the Meeting Point conference rooms; the guest rooms were also completely refurbished. Although all 20 rooms are open-plan in design no two rooms are the same. The Restaurant naturally forms the central focus of the Hanner. Here, too, clarity of form is the watchword, allowing all efforts to be channelled in the most important direction of all – the cuisine.

above:
Lobby
mid:
Restaurant

below:
Restaurant

above:
Restaurant-window with
view into Helen's valley
below:
Terrace

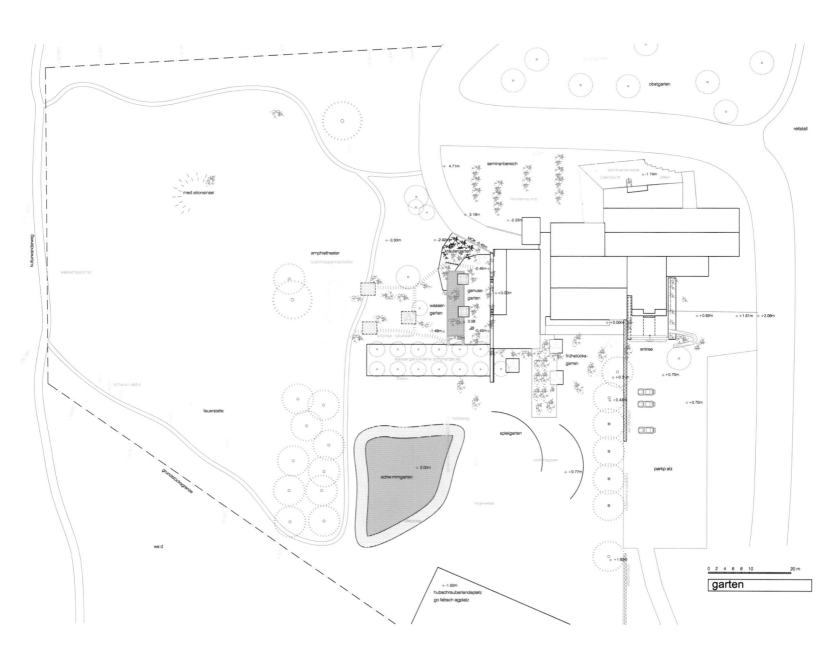

above:
Plan of garden
below:
Detail restaurant

above and below:
Guest rooms

Architecture:
W + R Leuenberger
**Interior Design
(plan):**
Lian Maria Bauer
**Interior Design
(details):**
André Furter
Sec Design

above:
Exterior view
below:
Portal Elements
with vestibule
right:
Entrance hall with
curved wall

Meisterschwanden
Hotel Seerose Elements

The full name of the Hotel Seerose on Hallwiler Lake, located far from the bustle of urban centers, speaks for itself. The interior of the hotel is an architectural expression of the four elements in colour and form and includes a number of surprising details. The fiery orange and structure painting of the arching wall of the reception area distinguishes itself from the walnut wood reception counter on the opposite side. Deep flame-coloured tones predominate in the Samui-Thai Restaurant. Earthenware-potted palms and sculptures manufactured to order in Thailand interrupt the severe architecture. The flowing grain of the zebrano wood fittings against the bamboo floor background underscores the Water theme on the first floor. The Earth element is represented by the dark wenge of the floor and veneer furniture and the saffron and cayenne colours. Deliberate stylistic statements come in the form of two-sided mirrors and steel handles on safe and bar. The gallery rooms of the top floor, with light flooding through their large windows, provide the link to the theme of Air. Each of the three honeymoon suites in the Hotel tower are designed along separate themes, infused with Thai or baroque flavour.

above:
Winter garden lounge
mid:
Brick vaults in wine cellar
"Solaia" with walk-in
glass cube
above right:
Ground plan ground floor

below left:
Restaurant
below right:
Restaurant Samui-Thai
with relief fountain and
metal torch

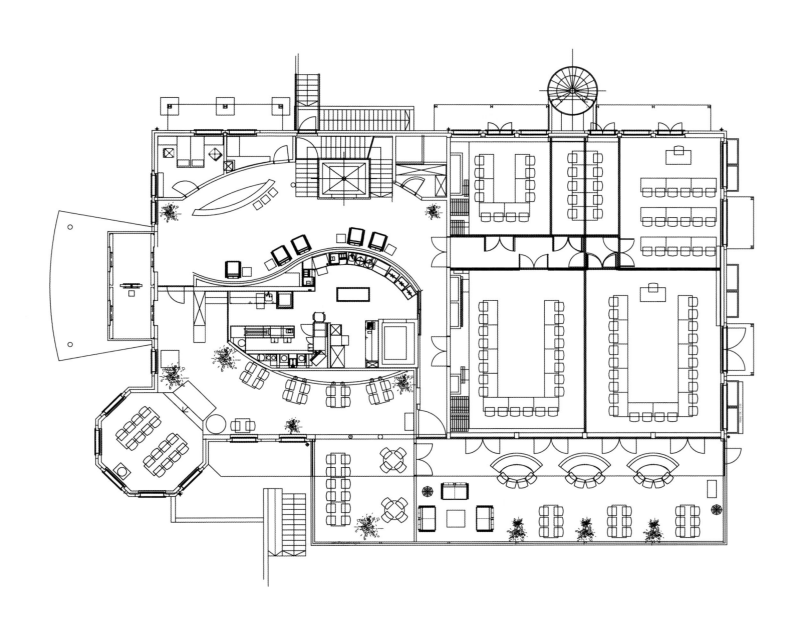

above:
Water room "Laguna" with
open bathroom
mid:
Air room "Luce" and
earth room "Cayenne"

below:
Water room "Cascade"

above:
Thai suite "Lotus"
with whirlpool
mid:
Dream suite "Baroque"
with four-poster bed
below:
Tower suite "Calypso" with
round bed under glass spire

Architecture:
Atelier d'Architecture
Hofmann
Interior Design:
AdP Décoration SA,
Dominique Couture

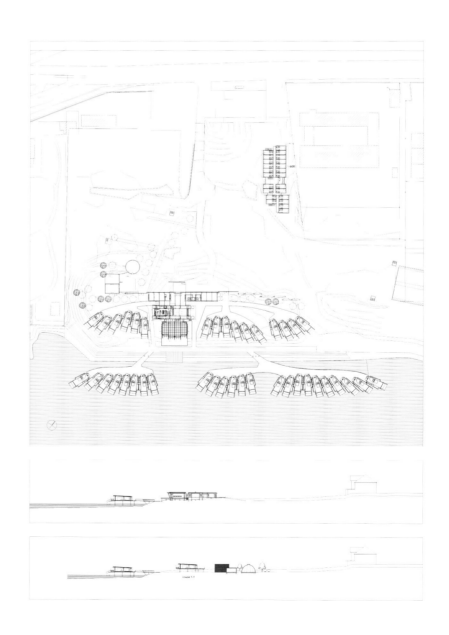

above and right:
Pavilions
below:
Site plan and views

Neuchâtel

What began as a project for Expo 2000, constructed in a record-breaking six months

Hotel Palafitte

and earmarked for complete eradication from the 15,000 km² area of public land two years later, is still standing today. There are two aspects to the success story that is the Hotel Palafitte: its extraordinary location and its design. From its location on – and along with 24 of the 40 pavilions in – Lake Neuchâtel the hotel offers guests a breathtaking view across the water to the snowy peaks of the Alpine panorama. As the name suggests (pala fitta, lat. = stake construction) half of the pavilion rests on posts above the surface of the lake, thus continuing an architectural tradition going back 5,000 years. Wood and glass predominate, allowing the building to harmonize well with the natural environment. The water is visible through the glass plating of the floor and light penetrates the roof of wooden and glass filigree. Computer-controlled technology in the pavilions are the buildings' concession to the modern age. The prize-winning ecological design gives precedence to the idea of sustainability and consists of methane gas fermenting plant, combustion engine and solar energy technology.

above:
Hotel entrance
mid:
Reception

below:
Bar

above and mid:
View of bar,
restaurant and lake
below:
Restaurant

above, mid and below:
Pavilions Lacustre

above:
Pavilion entrance
mid:
Pavilion interior
below:
Bathroom

Portraits
Architects

Prof. Fred Angerer · Gerald Hadler
Diplomingenieure Architekten

Müllerstrasse 42
D–80469 Munich
T +49.89.23 55 526
F +49.89.26 04 887
www.archah.com

Fred Angerer studied architecture at the Technical University in Munich, where he taught from 1968 to 1993 following freelance activities and postdoctoral qualification. Since 1994 he has realised diverse award-winning projects. Gerald Hadler (*1964) studied architecture at the Technical University in Munich and worked as a freelancer in several architecture agencies on award-winning projects. The Angerer & Hadler agency has been in business since 1995.

Lian Maria Bauer
Project Design

Seestrasse 18
CH–8800 Thalwil / Zurich
T +41.44.772 37 83
F +41.44.772 37 82
mail@lian-maria-bauer.com
www.lian-maria-bauer.com

Lian Maria Bauer (born 1956) completed a degree as a designer in Munich before working as an independent designer in the areas of Set Design for Film and Photo Production, Exhibitions and Event Design. She has been living in Switzerland since 1998 and working amongst other areas on interior design concepts for hotels and restaurants.

Behles + Partners Architects

Münsterhof 14
CH–8001 Zurich
T +41.44.221 21 26
F +41.44.212 05 26
behlespartner.architekten@everyware.ch

Wolfgang Behles (*1929) (photo right), architect BSA SWB VSI studied at the ETH Zurich and founded his architecture firm more than 40 years ago. Since 2001 the architects HTL Heinz Rutishauer (*1947) and Martin Hauser (*1964) (photo left) who have worked for him for many years joined as partners. They successfully lead the firm, setting the focus on the construction and conversions of hotels, with a special emphasis on the wellness sector.

Sigrid Bock, Architect

Salvador-Allende-Strasse 67
D–12559 Berlin
T / F +49.30.65 42 570
Hotel „Zur Bleiche": +49.35603.620

Sigrid Bock (*1953) completed her course of studies at the University for Architecture and Construction in Weimar. She worked as an architect for, among others, the German Interhotels in the Building / Design department, where she was responsible for all matters involved in the redesigning of existing hotels. In 2000 she founded her own agency. Since 2002, she has also worked as an architect for the "Zur Bleiche" Hotel in Burg / Spreewald.

bost berlin -
Interior Design . Architecture
Tassilo Bost

Danckelmannstrasse 9
D–14059 Berlin
T +49.30.30 12 11 14
F +49.30.30 12 11 17
info@bost-interieurdesign.de
www.bost-interieurdesign.de

Tassilo Bost studied at the Kassel Art Academy from 1975 to 1977; from 1977 to 1978 he studied Construction Drawing and Illustration under Prof. Hillmann before he went to the College for Design in Hamburg in 1978. Since 1988 Tassilo Bost is an independent designer with an office for Interior Design / Architecture where the main emphasis is on Hotel Design. Winner of the european Hotel-design award 2004.

Ralph Barenbrock

Bernhard-Seitz-Weg 15
D–18347 Ostseebad Ahrenshoop
T +49.38220.827 30
F +49.38220.827 33
info@ralphbarenbrock.de
www.ralphbarenbrock.de

Ralph Barenbrock (born 1947) studied architecture at the TU Braunschweig, before he worked for different architecture practices for several years and as a self-employed architect in Braunschweig. He has been the Managing Director of Elisabeth von Eicken since 1999. Since 2003 he has been continuing his activities as a freelance architect with main emphasis on the redevelopment of old buildings from Ahrenshoop.

Prof. Günther Domenig

Jahngasse 9
A–8010 Graz
T +43.316.82 77 53
F +43.316.82 77 539
office@domenig.at
www.domenig.at

Günter Domenig, born 1934, studied architecture at the TU Graz. In 1973 he founded own architecture practices in Graz, Klagenfurt and Vienna. He taught at the TU Graz from 1980 to 2000. Along with many awards Domenig received the Golden Cross of Honour 1st Class for Science and Art, the Golden Lion from the 9th Architectural Biennale in Venice and the Great Austrian State Price in 2004 alone.

Bernd Elfers
Interior Designer

Rockwinkeler Heerstrasse 107 B
D–28355 Bremen
T +49.421.25 26 32
F +49.421.205 33 63
bernd.elfers@arcor.de

Bernd Elfers (*1940) studied interior design at the FH in Hannover. Working for many years for Knoll International he was involved in numerous international projects. In 1971 he founded his own firm that focusses on planing and building residential and commercial buildings as well as hotels in Europe, Israel, the United Arab Emirates, Monte-negro. He won several awards, such as his design for the Deutsche Telekom shops.

Flum Design

Goldbek Platz 2
D–22303 Hamburg
T +49.40.27 16 36 60
F +49.40.27 16 36 61
flumdesign@flumdesign.de

Ralph Flum (*1956) studied architecture and furniture design at the academy of fine art in Pesaro (Italy). The company Flum Design, founded in 1985, developed out of a collaboration between father and son Flum while working together on the Elysée hotel in Hamburg. The main focus of their work is on hotel projects as well als luxury residences.

Hans Peter Fontana & Partners

Via Nova 14 | Postfach 91
CH–7017 Flims Dorf
T +41.81.911 16 42
F +41.81.911 20 93
info@fontana-und-partner.ch
www.fontana-und-partner.ch

Hans Peter Fontana (*1960) studied architecture at the Winterthur Technical Institute and founded an architect's office in 1984, as well as the construction company Plaunca Sulegl. He also studied Construction and Power at the AT Chur in 1988 and in 1995 Aspects of Construction Ecology at the TWI. His main areas of work are amongst others the areas of House Building, Commercial Construction, Tourism and Infrastructure Construction as well as Construction Management.

Décoration Jacques Garcia

212, rue de Rivoli
F–75001 Paris
T +33.1.42 97 48 70
F +33.1.42 97 48 10

Jacques Garcia, born 1947, studied Interior Design at the ESAG Penninghen in Paris. His "public" career began with the renovation of the Hotel Royal in Deauville. Since then amongst others, the Hôtel Majestic in Cannes, the Hôtel Costes Paris, as well as projects all over the world belong to his works. He was honoured for his work with the title Chevalier de la Légion d'honneur in 1995.

Karen Heldmann

Rosenstrasse 38
D–70182 Stuttgart
T +49.711.23 77 770
F +49.711.23 77 775
kontakt@zauberlehrling.de
www.zauberlehrling.de

Karen Heldman (*1962), a hotel professional, opened with her husband the restaurant Zauberlehrling (magician apprentice) in Stuttgart. When adding hotel facilities to it in 2001/2002 she developed the entire design – the furnishing, lights, colours – and conducted the implementation.

Atelier d'Architecture Hofmann

Avenue de l'universite 9–11
CH–1005 Lausanne
T +41.21.323 75 45
F +41.21.323 75 44
info@k-hofmann.ch

Kurt Hoffmann (born 1944) was included in the Swiss register of Architects and Engineers REG-A in 1985 and has been running his own architecture practice in Lausanne since 1970. The main themes of his work are housing and hotel construction, as well as alternative agriculture constructions.

Klemens Hüls
Planning Office Hüls

Marktallee 63
D–48165 Münster
T +49.2501.96 40 400
F +49.2501.96 40 406
info@planungsbuero-huels.de

Born in Bocholt in 1959, Klemens Hüls completed his architectural studies in Detmold. Afterwards he had a managing function in different architecture practices. In 1999 he founded his own planning office, which develops integrated interior and graphic design concepts focussed on marketing and specific target groups.

Jaggi & Partners

Palacestrasse 1
CH–3780 Gstaad
T +41.33.744 26 88
F +41.33.744 59 72
jaggi-partner@bluewin.ch

Stephan Jaggi (*1947) studied interior design at the state academy of fine arts in Stuttgart. He founded his own architure and design firm in Gstaad, Switzerland in 1979. His focus is the construction and conversion of hotels, the design of restaurants and stores as well as private chalets and villas in Switzerland, Germany and Mallorca.

k/h
Office for Interior Design and Design
Harald Klein | Bert Haller

An der Eickesmühle 30
D–41238 Mönchengladbach
T +49.2166.94 630
F +49.2166.94 6322
design@klein-haller.de
www.klein-haller.de

The designer Harald Klein (*1953) and the interior designer Bert Haller (*1956) have been working together since 1998 under the name k/h. Their projects tend to focus on gastronomy and hotels. Along with the creation of interior design concepts, they also develop business ideas and corporate design, budget proposals and light- and furnishing plans.

Prof. Josef Paul Kleihues

Helmholtzstrasse 42
D–10587 Berlin
T +49.30.399 799 0
F +49.30.399 799 77
berlin@kleihues.com
www.kleihues.com

Josef Paul Kleihues (1933–2004) studied in Berlin and Paris. He himself characterises his understanding of architecture as "poetic rationalism", a pronounced rationalistic approach coupled with artistic imagination. The architectural firm Kleihues + Kleihues, founded in 1996 by his son Jan Kleihues and Norbert Hensel, which is based on the architectural bureau by Josef Paul Kleihues from 1962, just finished the Maritim and the Concorde Hotel in Berlin.

Kochta Architects

Cuvillies Strasse 11
D–81679 Munich
T +49.89.92 801 0
F +49.89.92 801 140
h.kochta@kochta-architekten.de
www.kochta-architekten.de

Herbert Kochta (*1932) studied architecture at the Technical University in Munich and the Royal Academy in Stockholm. Following many years of practical activity in architecture agencies in Berlin, Vienna and Munich, he founded his own office in 1960. Herbert Kochta was a member of the Civic Commission of Munich, State Chairman of the BDA (Federation of German Architects) in Bavaria and member of the board of the Bavarian Chamber of Architects.

Architecture Practice
Andreas Krainer

Konradweg 3
A–9020 Klagenfurt
T +43.463.21 82 58
F +43.463.21 82 22
studio@krainerarchitect.at

Andreas Krainer (*1952) studied architecture at the Technical University of Graz. The Krainer architecture agency has existed in Klagenfurt since 1985. Areas of activity include complete architectural services ranging from the invitation to tender through the planning to project supervision, as well as construction supervision of projects on location in the most diverse areas.

Lindner Architects

Emanuel-Leutze-Strasse 17
D–40547 Düsseldorf
T +49.211.52 820
F +49.211.52 82412
info@lindner-architekten.de
www.lindnder-architekten.de

After completing his architectural studies in Idstein / Taunus and Wuppertal, and then managing a construction department for seven years, Otto Lindner started a firm of Architects in Neuss, as a self-employed architect. Gebau AG also founded by Lindner has since 1965 been designing and implementing projects as a contracting company for the Deutsche Apotheker- und Ärztebank with an investment volume of 2.5 billion euros to date.

**Meierhofer Grob
Architecture Planning Advisory**

Caplania
CH–7031 Laax
T +41.81.921 51 17
F +41.81.921 51 26
arch.meierhofer@bluewin.ch

Madeleine Grob (*1955) earned her diploma as a cultural engineer at the ETHZ (Swiss Federal Institute of Technology in Zurich). Prior to the cooperation with René Meierhofer in 2001 she was for many years employee and partner in an engineering and surveying office. René Meierhofer (*1945) studied at the polytechnic in Winterthur and operated his own office until 2000. All as-pects of projects in the areas of design, construction and planning are realized in cooperation.

Mescherowsky Architects

Theaterstrasse 17
D–52062 Aachen
T +49.241.477 81 0
F +49.241.477 81 11
info@mescherowsky.de
www.mescherowsky.de

Gregor Mescherowsky studied architecture at the Technical University in Berlin and founded the Mescherowsky Architects BDA agency in 1990. In 1995 he also opened the mtbauplan GmbH together with Udo Thiemann, with fields of activity including construction site management, account, schedule and project control. He participated in urban planning projects in The Hague and Lüttich, among others, and worked for two years in the Rem Koolhaas office for two years.

**Sabine Mescherowsky
Interior Design**

Oelschlägerstrasse 65–67
D–47798 Krefeld
T +49.2151.36 58 4 0
F +49.2151.36 58 4 11
info@innenarchitektur-SAM.de
www.sabinemescherowsky.de

Sabine Mescherowsky (born 1962) studied interior design at Düsseldorf University of Applied Sciences. She has been working as an independent interior designer since 1989, the Sabine Mescherowsky office in Krefeld has been in existence since 2001. Her European wide projects are in the areas of hotel, gastronomy, wellness, residential design, office and shop concepts, rehabilitation and care facilities, as well as private houses.

MKV Design

229-231 High Holborn
UK–London, WC1V 7DA
T +44.207.24 22 466
F +44.207.24 22 488
info@mkvdesign.com
www.mkvdesign.com

MKV Design was founded in 1999 in London by Maria Vafiadis, who had studied architecture and interior design in Milan, Vienna, Athens and London. During this time she managed projects in the Luxury Hotel Sector in the whole of Europe. MKV Design is made up of 17 people today with projects in amongst other places Croatia, Spain, Greece, Russia, Poland and Austria.

Ateliers Jean Nouvel

10 Cité d'Angoulême
F–75011 Paris
T +33.1.49 23 83 83
F +33.1.43 14 81 10
info@jeannouvel.fr
www.jeannouvel.fr

Jean Nouvel, born 1945 in Fumel, France has managed his own architect's office since 1970. The star architect who has been awarded many international prizes (e.g. the gold medal from the French Academy of Architecture, and the Japanese Praemium Imperiale 2005). His works cover amongst other things the Opera House in Lyon, the Fondation Cartier in Paris and the Dentsu Tower in Tokyo.

**Selvaggio S.A.
Carlo Rampazzi, Interior Design**

Vicolo Ghiriglioni 3
CH–6612 Ascona
T +41.91.785 19 10
F +41.91.785 19 19
info@selvaggio.ch
www.selvaggio.ch

Carlo Rampazzi was born in 1949 in Acona. He gained his diploma for Interior Design and Interior Decoration in Lugano, his specialisation followed in Paris. In the early eighties Rampazzi began to develop his own Interior Design Collections that he regularly exhibits at internationally known furniture trade fairs, for example in Milan.

Architecture Practice Oana Rosen

Westendstrasse 46
D–60325 Frankfurt / Main
T +49.69.97 40 57 68
F +49.69.71 40 29 58
OanaRosen@t-online.de

Oana Rosen studied Interior Design as well as Architecture in Darmstadt. After working for several years both as an employed and self-employed architect, she founded her own office in 1995. The main fields of work are conversion, renovation and redesign of office buildings, as well as conversions and extensions of high quality living accommodation.

**Thomas Rudolf
Freelance Architect**

Brunnenweg 8
D–72622 Nürtingen
T +49.7022.70 87 00
F +49.7022.70 87 08
info@architekt-rudolf.de
www.architekt-rudolf.de

Born in 1960 in Stuttgart Thomas Rudolf studied at the College of Architecture there, specialising in Town Planning. After working in various architecture practices as self-employed, he became independent in 1994. In recent years he has specialised in renovations, redevelopment and building maintenance.

Pia M. Schmid
Architektur & Designbüro

Augustinergasse 25
CH–8001 Zurich
T +41.1.221 08 48
F +41.1.221 08 49
archpiaschmid@into.ch
www.piaschmid.com

Before her architecture education Pia
Schmid studied at the film-school in
Berlin. In 1980 she founded her own
architecture firm with a main focus on
the hotel sector, gastronony, wellness
as well as public building in Switzerland and abroad. Her work is always a
composition that creates a synthesis of
a precise analysis and the creative
space that develops out of it. Her latest
project is a hotel-boat on the river Nile.

Karsten Schmidt-Hoensdorf

Heinrichstrasse 267
CH–8005 Zurich
T +41.44.463 12 33
F +41.66.463 35 07
www.ida14.ch

Karsten Schmidt-Hoensdorf (*1956)
initially studied history and political
science in Munich and Toulouse before
turning to architecture. Following his
architecture studies he founded his
own office in 1993 with a focus on interior decoration and design. He thereby
primarily concentrated on the gastronomy / hotel industries as well as art
and culture.

Rainer Seiferth Architect

Hagelberger Strasse 18
D–10965 Berlin
T +49.30.692 42 42
F +49.30.691 23 56
seiferth@ngi.de
www.rainerseiferth.com

Rainer Seiferth (*1955) studied in
Berlin at the HDK (University of the
Arts) and has worked as a freelance
architect in Berlin since 1986. The individual office looks after all service
phases of planning and construction,
with the focus on the reanimation of
neglected residential and industrial
objects. These are evident, for example, in the Kalkscheune Berlin and in
Berlin inner city areas.

HEP Simon Architect
Simon + Partners Architects

Schönhauser Allee 149
D–10435 Berlin
T +49.30.44 300 730
F +49.30.44 300 731
office@simon-partner.com
www.simon-partner-architekten.de

HEP Simon (born 1950) studied architecture and experimental environmen-
tal design in Braunschweig. Until 1983
he was an academic assistant in the
Architectural Department at the TU
Braunschweig, before he founded the
architecture practice Simon & Partners
in Braunschweig. Extended by a Berlin
branch in 1995, the office realises projects in the areas of change of use and
redevelopment of buildings.

Tilla Theus and Partners

Bionstrasse 18
CH–8006 Zurich
T +41.1.363 42 12
F +41.1.361 07 94
info@tillatheus.ch
www.tillatheus.ch

Dipl. Arch. ETH/SIA/BSA Tilla Theus
(*1943) specialises in project management and the execution of new building
in the superior town planning context,
in conversions and renovations of listed
buildings, as well as interior design
and room design. She has been honoured by the City of Zurich numerous
times, most recently for the total renovation of the Mythenquai in Zurich.

Matteo Thun

Via Appiani 9
I–20121 Milano
T +39.02.65 56 911
F +39.02.65 70 646
info@matteothun.com
www.matteothun.com

Matteo Thun (b. 1952) has owned his
own studio since 1984 and is a member
of the "Milan School". He avoids identi-
fication with a single style, looking
instead for the suitable strategy to
apply to each individual client. This is
reflected in his credo "Echo, not ego".
He aims at creating "products whose
technical and aesthetic quality will
stand the test of time both in their
detail and their broad features".

Tombusch & Brumann

Rohlmanns Hof | Lüdinghauser Str. 3
D–59387 Ascheberg
T +49.25.93 95 560
F +49.25.93 95 5649
www.tombusch-brumann.de

Tombusch & Brumann GmbH is one of
the leading service companies in the
area of hotel interior design. The cus-
tomer is supplied with tailored, innovative hotel interior design concepts from
design to production. Creative room
worlds are produced, planned profes-
sionally and implemented in line with
the location, the local conditions, and
the special requirements of the guests.

UN Studio
Ben van Berkel, Caroline Bos

Stadhouderskade 113
NL–1073 AX Amsterdam
T +31.20.57 02 040
F +31.20.57 02 041
info@unstudio.com
www.unstudio.com

UN Studio was founded in December
1998 by Ben van Berkel and Caroline
Bos. The partners have already carried
out projects together since 1988,
amongst others the Aedes East Gallery
for Kristin Freireiss in Berlin and the
Erasmus Bridge in Rotterdam. Current
projects cover the design of the new
Mercedes Benz Museum in Stuttgart
as well as the new design of the har-
bour in Genoa.

Hotel Index

Aenea Designhotel www.aenea.at **104**
Arabella Sheraton Bogenhausen www.arabellasheraton.com **266**
Arte Luise Kunsthotel www.luise-berlin.com **92**
Atlantic Hotel Galopprennbahn www.atlantic-hotels.de **236**
Augarten Hotel www.augartenhotel.com **110**

Bristol Hotel www.bristol-hotel.de **248**
Der Teufelhof www.teufelhof.com **122**
Dorint Sofitel Bayerpost www.dorint.de **34**
Dorint Sofitel Söl'ring Hof www.sofitel.com **298**
Hanner Restaurant Hotel www.hanner.cc **310**
Hotel Castell www.hotelcastell.ch **84**
Hôtel des Trois Couronnes www.hoteltroiscouronnes.ch **178**
Hotel Drei Raben www.hotel-drei-raben.de **278**
Hotel Eden Roc www.edenroc.ch **154**
Hotel Elephant www.luxurycollection.com **22**
Hotel Elisabeth von Eicken www.elisabethvoneicken.de **292**
Hotel Imperial www.luxurycollection.com **148**
Hotel Landhaus Wachtelhof www.wachtelhof.de **198**
Hotel Madlein www.ischglmadlein.com **54**
Hotel Misani www.hotelmisani.ch **78**
Hotel Palafitte www.palafitte.ch **322**
Hotel Restaurant Ritzi www.hotel-ritzi.de **272**
Hotel Schloss Neuhardenberg www.schlossneuhardenberg.de **16**
Hotel Seerose Elements www.seerose.ch **316**
Inn Side Premium Hotel www.innside.de **242**
Inter Continental Resort Berchtesgaden www.ichotelsgroup.com **48**
Kloster Hornbach www.kloster-hornbach.de **28**
La Réserve Hotel & Spa www.lareserve.ch **216**
Landhaus Stricker www.landhaus-stricker.de **304**
Lausanne Palace & Spa www.lausanne-palace.com **172**
Lenkerhof Alpine Resort www.lenkerhof.ch **222**
Mandarin Oriental Hotel du Rhône www.mandarinoriental.com **160**
Mövenpick Hotel Berlin www.moevenpick-berlin.com **10**
Park Hotel Waldhaus www.parkhotel-waldhaus.ch **60**
Pflaums Posthotel www.ppp.com **98**
Radisson SAS Hotel www.radisson.com **254**
Riders Palace www.riderspalace.ch **72**
Rogner Bad Blumau Hotel & Spa www.blumau.com **204**
Romantic-Hotel Chesa Grischuna www.chesagrischuna.ch **66**
Schwarzer Adler www.adlerkitz.at **210**
Style Hotel Vienna www.stylehotel.at **116**
The Hotel www.the-hotel.ch **128**
The Regent www.regenthotels.com **136**
The Westin Bellevue www.westin-bellevue.com **142**
The Westin Leipzig www.starwoodhotels.com **260**
Therme Vals www.therme-vals.ch **228**
Victoria-Jungfrau Grand Hotel & Spa www.victoria-jungfrau.ch **166**
Widder Hotel www.widder.ch **40**
Yachthafenresidenz Hohe Düne www.yhd.de **186**
Zauberlehrling www.zauberlehrling.de **284**
Zur Bleiche Resort & Spa www.hotel-zur-bleiche.com **192**

© Archiv Hotel Imperial 148–153 | © Augarten Hotel, Graz 110–115 | © Dorint Sofitel Söl'ring Sylt 298–303 | © Elfers Interior Architecture 242–247 | © Family Clausing 192–197 | © Hanner Hotel 310–315 | © HOCHTIEF Projektentwicklung GmbH, Rhein-Main 255 | © Hotel Trois Couronnes 178–183 | © Hundertwasser Architekturprojekt 204–209 | © InterConti

Picture Credits / Further Participants

Berchtesgaden 48, 50 below, 51 above left and below, 52–53 | © LaRezia Verwaltungen AG 78–83 | © Lausanne Palace & Spa 172–177 | © Mandarin Oriental Geneva 160–165 | © Park Hotel Waldhaus Flims 60 | © Radisson SAS Hotel Frankfurt 254, 256–259 | © Rampazzi 154–159 | © The Hotel Lucerne 128–133 | © The Regent 144–147 | © Therme Vals 229, 231 | © Tilla Theus and Partners 40–45 | © Westin Bellevue Dresden 142 above | © WSF Boutiquehotel Betriebsgesellschaft mbH 116–121 | © Yacht-hafenresidenz Hohe Düne GmbH 186–191 | Ammann, Friedel 122–127 | Andersen, Bernd 201 below | Apostoloidis, George 160–165 | Astis Krause 20 above | Barradi, Robert 216 below, 221 | Bertin, F. 322–327 | Bioret, Jean-Patrik 172 above | Born, Geri 62 mid, 63 left | Braun, Zooey 278–283 | Brée, Christian 92 above, 94–95, 96 above and below, 97 | Bühler, Michael, Zurich 61 | Bumann, G. 34–35 | Danuser, Gaudenz 62 above and below, 63 mid and right, 64, 65 above and mid, 72–77 | Eidenmüller, Bernd 284–285, 287–289 | Fiorito, Massimo: 49, 50 above, 51 above right | Flak, Andrea 10–11 below, 14–15 | Fotostudio Frigesch Lampelmeyer 210–215 | Gardette, Gregoire 216 above, 217, 218–219, 220, 221 | Greuner, Sebastian 10 above, 12–13 | Grünig, Christoph "Stöh", Biel 316–321 | Guntli, Reto 68 below | Gyger, Marcus 168, 169 above, mid, below left, 171 above, mid | Hamel, Matthias 24 above and mid, 27 above, 260 above, 265, 267 above | Hansen, Hagen 292–297 | Helfenstein, Heinrich 232–233 | Jaussi, Michel 66, 69, 71 | Klocke Verlag 286 | Komossa, Jens 92–93 below, 96 mid | Krischker, Gerhard 166–167, 169 below right, 170, 171 below | KSH Hotelbetriebs GmbH 272–277 | Lokie, Steve 198–200, 201 above, 202–203 | Marten Burde and Ydo Sol 98–103 | McBride, Simon 68 above, 70 | Miller, Robert 116–121 | Muhs, Andreas 22–23, 24 below, 25, 26, 27 below, 260–261 below, 262–264 | Müller, Stephan 136–137 | Oberli, Andreas 67 | Quabbe + Tessmann 143–147 | Reinhard, Michael 222–227 | Richters, Christian 84–89 | Roosen, Dieter 248–253 | Rumpf, Brigitte, Fotoatelier Tollinger, Klagenfurt 328 second photo from left | Rupa, Dolores 65 below | Soenne 36–39, 54–59, 104–109, 236–241 | Spans, Gerd 28–33 | Spiluttini, Margherita 228, 230 | Starwood Hotels & Resorts Worldwide, Inc. 266–267, 268 below, 269–271 | Toma Babovic 16–19, 20 below, 21 | Vonow, Karin and Ammon, Emanuel 78–83 | Wiesenhofer, Hans 204–209

Mövenpick Hotel Berlin, near Potsdamer Platz | page 10–15
GKK & Partners | Greschik Gutmann Kuhlen, Berlin
BIG Bau- und Ingenieurgesell-schaft mbH, Herten

Hotel Castell Zuoz | page 84–89
Staff member UN Studio: Pablo Rica and Sebastian Schaeffer with Andrew Benn, Claudia Dorner, Dag Thies, Peter Irmscher, Albert Gnodde, Martin Kuitert, Ron Roos, Eric den Eerzamen, Marco Hemmerling, Ergian Alberg, Peter Trummer, Sophie Valla, Tiago Nunes, Tina Bayerl, Peter Jorgensen

Arte Luise Kunsthotel | page 92–97
Elvira Bach, Bananensprayer Th. Baumgärtel, Stefan Jung, Dieter Finke, Oliver Jordan, Wolfgang Petrick, Dieter Mammel, Jo Oberhäuser, Shukhrat Babadjan, Ulrike Arnold, Manfred Heckmann, Helmut Löhr, Peter Mönnig, Rainer Gross, Volker März, Heiner Meyer, Kiddy Citny, Guido Sieber, Ottmar Hörl, A. Paeslack, Könige d. Herzen, M. Linnenbrink, Nina Fasoulido, Angela Dwyer, Sabine Groß, Kehl, Odin, Stefan Bree, Silke, Vollmers, Peter Buechler, Tine Benz, B. Schroeck, Carlos Manrique, Roman Schmelter, Eva Castringus, J. J. Anniroc, Sabine Hartung, Christoph Platz, Vera Leutlhoff, Norbert Thiel, ADOCHI, Hans v. Meeuwen, Andreas, Silbermann, Schmiddem. Moritz Götze, Goran Djurovic

Zur Bleiche Resort & Spa | page 192–197
Offenstein Relax Architecture, Munich | Architecture Practice Wetzk, Limberg | Engineer Office Kollosche, Burg im Spreewald

Hotel Index

Aenea Designhotel   www.aenea.at **104**
Arabella Sheraton Bogenhausen   www.arabellasheraton.com **266**
Arte Luise Kunsthotel   www.luise-berlin.com **92**
Atlantic Hotel Galopprennbahn   www.atlantic-hotels.de **236**
Augarten Hotel   www.augartenhotel.com **110**

Bristol Hotel   www.bristol-hotel.de **248**
Der Teufelhof   www.teufelhof.com **122**
Dorint Sofitel Bayerpost   www.dorint.de **34**
Dorint Sofitel Söl'ring Hof   www.sofitel.com **298**
Hanner Restaurant Hotel   www.hanner.cc **310**
Hotel Castell   www.hotelcastell.ch **84**
Hôtel des Trois Couronnes   www.hoteltroiscouronnes.ch **178**
Hotel Drei Raben   www.hotel-drei-raben.de **278**
Hotel Eden Roc   www.edenroc.ch **154**
Hotel Elephant   www.luxurycollection.com **22**
Hotel Elisabeth von Eicken   www.elisabethvoneicken.de **292**
Hotel Imperial   www.luxurycollection.com **148**
Hotel Landhaus Wachtelhof   www.wachtelhof.de **198**
Hotel Madlein   www.ischglmadlein.com **54**
Hotel Misani   www.hotelmisani.ch **78**
Hotel Palafitte   www.palafitte.ch **322**
Hotel Restaurant Ritzi   www.hotel-ritzi.de **272**
Hotel Schloss Neuhardenberg   www.schlossneuhardenberg.de **16**
Hotel Seerose Elements   www.seerose.ch **316**
Inn Side Premium Hotel   www.innside.de **242**
Inter Continental Resort Berchtesgaden   www.ichotelsgroup.com **48**
Kloster Hornbach   www.kloster-hornbach.de **28**
La Réserve Hotel & Spa   www.lareserve.ch **216**
Landhaus Stricker   www.landhaus-stricker.de **304**
Lausanne Palace & Spa   www.lausanne-palace.com **172**
Lenkerhof Alpine Resort   www.lenkerhof.ch **222**
Mandarin Oriental Hotel du Rhône   www.mandarinoriental.com **160**
Mövenpick Hotel Berlin   www.moevenpick-berlin.com **10**
Park Hotel Waldhaus   www.parkhotel-waldhaus.ch **60**
Pflaums Posthotel   www.ppp.com **98**
Radisson SAS Hotel   www.radisson.com **254**
Riders Palace   www.riderspalace.ch **72**
Rogner Bad Blumau Hotel & Spa   www.blumau.com **204**
Romantic-Hotel Chesa Grischuna   www.chesagrischuna.ch **66**
Schwarzer Adler   www.adlerkitz.at **210**
Style Hotel Vienna   www.stylehotel.at **116**
The Hotel   www.the-hotel.ch **128**
The Regent   www.regenthotels.com **136**
The Westin Bellevue   www.westin-bellevue.com **142**
The Westin Leipzig   www.starwoodhotels.com **260**
Therme Vals   www.therme-vals.ch **228**
Victoria-Jungfrau Grand Hotel & Spa   www.victoria-jungfrau.ch **166**
Widder Hotel   www.widder.ch **40**
Yachthafenresidenz Hohe Düne   www.yhd.de **186**
Zauberlehrling   www.zauberlehrling.de **284**
Zur Bleiche Resort & Spa   www.hotel-zur-bleiche.com **192**

Picture Credits / Further Participants

Mövenpick Hotel Berlin, near Potsdamer Platz | page 10–15
GKK & Partners | Greschik Gutmann Kuhlen, Berlin
BIG Bau- und Ingenieurgesellschaft mbH, Herten

Hotel Castell Zuoz | page 84–89
Staff member UN Studio: Pablo Rica and Sebastian Schaeffer with Andrew Benn, Claudia Dorner, Dag Thies, Peter Irmscher, Albert Gnodde, Martin Kuitert, Ron Roos, Eric den Eerzamen, Marco Hemmerling, Ergian Alberg, Peter Trummer, Sophie Valla, Tiago Nunes, Tina Bayerl, Peter Jorgensen

Arte Luise Kunsthotel | page 92–97
Elvira Bach, Bananensprayer Th. Baumgärtel, Stefan Jung, Dieter Finke, Oliver Jordan, Wolfgang Petrick, Dieter Mammel, Jo Oberhäuser, Shukhrat Babadjan, Ulrike Arnold, Manfred Heckmann, Helmut Löhr, Peter Mönnig, Rainer Gross, Volker März, Heiner Meyer, Kiddy Citny, Guido Sieber, Ottmar Hörl, A. Paeslack, Könige d. Herzen, M. Linnenbrink, Nina Fasoulido, Angela Dwyer, Sabine Groß, Kehl, Odin, Stefan Bree, Silke, Vollmers, Peter Buechler, Tine Benz, B. Schroeck, Carlos Manrique, Roman Schmelter, Eva Castringus, J. J. Anniroc, Sabine Hartung, Christoph Platz, Vera Leutlhoff, Norbert Thiel, ADOCHI, Hans v. Meeuwen, Andreas, Silbermann, Schmiddem. Moritz Götze, Goran Djurovic

Zur Bleiche Resort & Spa | page 192–197
Offenstein Relax Architecture, Munich | Architecture Practice Wetzk, Limberg | Engineer Office Kollosche, Burg im Spreewald